SECOND BITE OF THE CHERRY

Eating for health and pleasure
—— in the middle years ——

Alan Stewart and Margaret Jackson

An OPTIMA book

First published 1988 by Sun Books
THE MACMILLAN COMPANY OF AUSTRALIA PTY LTD
107 Moray Street, South Melbourne 3205
6 Clarke Street, Crows Nest 2065

This edition published in 1988 by Macdonald Optima,
a division of Macdonald & Co. (Publishers) Ltd

A Pergamon Press plc Company

Stewart, Alan
    Second bite of the cherry.
    1. Health food dishes — Recipes
    I. Title II. Jackson, Margaret
    641.5'637

ISBN 0-356-15907-8

Macdonald & Co. (Publishers) Ltd
3rd Floor
Greater London House
Hampstead Road
London NWI 7QX

Set in Optima by Graphicraft Typesetters Ltd, Hong Kong
Printed in Hong Kong

Contents

To the Reader

If you want the chance to enjoy good health for the rest of your life, and do the things you've always wanted, then *Second Bite of the Cherry* is for you. It contains up-to-date scientific information on good nutrition and a wealth of cooking ideas and recipes to make healthy food choices easy choices. It is not, however, just a nutrition book nor is it just a cookery book.

This book is especially for those of you who are over forty years of age. These are the vital years, the time to be leading a life filled with 'passion, poems and magic'. This is also the time to take stock of the biological clock and do positive things to keep your body in good working order.

Three main themes weave through the book. Firstly, if you get your food right, other parts of your life will follow suit. Begin your fresh start by making changes to what you eat, using the guidelines and recipes in the following chapters and some remarkable consequences could follow — better health, new adventures and an ongoing sense of accomplishing 'one small triumph at a time'.

Secondly, variety is an essential ingredient in healthy eating. If your diet is based on foods rich in nutrients then you can enjoy the occasional indulgence food, such as your favourite pastry, without feeling guilty.

Thirdly, it's never too late to make changes to your lifestyle which will put you on the path to better health. It's always worth a go!

Chapter 1 examines the reasons why good nutrition is the foundation of vital living. It focuses on the powerful influence of food on your health, both now and in the future, and specifically, on the importance of good nutrition to prevent coronary heart disease and other health disorders. It also examines the role food can play in your self esteem and in your relationship with others. Have you ever thought of food as a medium for self expression or for getting to know someone?

Chapter 2 can be summed up in three words ... Healthy Diet Triangle (opposite page 33). This novel and practical guide provides you with a framework to make food choices which promote both good health and pleasurable eating. The

Triangle is based on up-to-date scientific and medical research which shows how important it is to concentrate on foods which are high in fibre and low in fat. How can you tell if you're eating enough fibre? What are some easy ways to cut down on the amount of fat you eat? You'll find the answers in this section.

Chapter 3 contains approximately one hundred nutritious, tasty and easy-to-prepare recipes. You will quickly discover that they are simple yet elegant. The ingredients are an interesting blend of the novel and the familiar to make healthy eating an enjoyable and adventurous experience. A unique feature of the recipes is that they are arranged in such a way that you can refer directly to the Healthy Diet Triangle when making food choices.

Chapter 4 focuses on some specific food and nutrition issues to help you implement the dietary guidelines in this book. They are arranged alphabetically for easy reference. Included are some handy hints on how to prepare different kinds of foods, such as fruit and vegetables, and what to look for on food labels to make you nutrition-wise in this shiny, electronic age. There is also information on weight control, the value of exercise, calcium, vitamin and mineral supplements and food additives.

The book evolved from a number of interesting connections. In the past few years Margaret Jackson has participated in projects with mothers of young families to increase their knowledge and skills in preparing nutritious foods and to widen their social contacts. Alan Stewart has undertaken similar activities with elderly people. Positive feedback and helpful suggestions also came from users of an earlier book co-authored by Alan, *Cooking for the Elderly: A Guide to Good Nutrition and Cuisine in Nursing Homes, Hostels and Hospitals* which was published in Australia in 1984 and a new edition was released in Britain in 1988 (Winslow Press, London).

If you put into practice the ideas in *Second Bite of the Cherry* you can expect to:

- Regain a zest for living.
- Feel better now than you have done for years.
- Improve your chances of keeping healthy in the future.

- Do something creative into which you can really project yourself and which you will find highly satisfying.

- Experiment with the cooking ideas in this book to have get-togethers with old friends as well as new acquaintances.

A successful fresh start in life comes from seeing things differently. Seeing things differently comes from doing things differently. Begin your new regime with some changes to your eating pattern and see what happens. You could be surprised at just how easy it is to 're-style' your life.

Acknowledgements

There are many people we would like to thank for the encouragement and contribution they made to this book, both in the early phase when it was a series of unstructured ideas and later, when the manuscript took shape and specific issues were addressed. There are too many people to name individually but there are some who must be especially singled out.

We would like to thank Anthea Krieg, nutritionist *extraordinaire*, who created the link between good recipes, good nutrition and good companionship. Also Burt Surmon, Ruth Stock and the research team on the 'Cooking and Cobbers' project, whose professionalism added another dimension — good management.

Alan Bentley of the Medical Illustration and Media Unit at the Flinders Medical Centre was responsible for the art work — attractive enough to launch any recipe.

Thank you also to our respective families for their encouragement and forbearance and to Sonia Jackson for proof reading much of the material.

We are greatly indebted to Vivien Stewart who helped impose a structure on the raw material, did much of the initial editing and contributed substantially to the creative writing.

Finally, we are especially grateful to Anne Deveson, Director of the Australian Film and Television School for so graciously writing the foreword.

Foreword

I grew up with a father who liked steak-and-kidney pudding, treacle tart, kippers and Stilton cheese. My mother's favourites were buttered Brazil nuts, chocolate soufflés and cheese fondues. They were both heavy smokers. Occasionally a prick of conscience or a shaft of indigestion would impel them towards a healthier life style, and my mother once embarked on something called the Hay Diet which disappointed me because it wasn't what it sounded like.

No, they didn't live till they were a hundred and four. They sniffled and wheezled their way through their sixties and seventies. My father ended up living off senna pods and porridge, and my mother had bad arthritis which she accepted as a normal consequence of old age.

I guess the point of these family revelations is that for people of my parents' generation, ill-health was certainly something you tried to prevent, but good health wasn't something you strove to attain. Non-smokers were non-fashionable. And people who regularly dieted were viewed with suspicion as they probably had other anti-social habits which they kept from view.

Now we know better. Now we are salt-conscious, cholesterol-conscious, muesli-munchers and calorie-counters. And often we are crashing bores. Which is why *Second Bite of the Cherry* is such a refreshing change from the normal run of health books, because it isn't obsessive, and it presents good health as a goal which is fun to achieve.

The book is easy to follow. I blank out at injunctions to weigh each portion or to juggle different food types in permutations which require a calculator. I'm an idiot at shopping which requires me to peer at the small print to spot the forbidden ingredients. I want to be healthy without turning my whole life upside down or becoming a social misfit because I can only eat boiled pears.

Healthy food doesn't have to be dreary food. It can be full of colour, flavour and variety. It can smell good and taste good. It can be lovingly produced in kitchens which are inviting and where people want to gather.

Second Bite of the Cherry has one, overriding appeal. It reminds us that good health means a good life, a chance to repair the damages of the past, and the promise of adventures in the years ahead.

Anne Deveson.

Anne Deveson

1
Food – the Key to Vital Living

Introduction

The food we eat has a powerful influence on us. It determines our physical and mental well being. A healthy eating pattern helps us feel well. It also enables us to take on new challenges and achieve goals we set for ourselves.

The aim of this book is to help you to broaden your perspective of the positive role food can play in your life and to find your own answer to the questions:

'What dividend can I expect from an investment of time and effort to understand the principles of good nutrition, to follow the dietary guidelines and to try the recipes in *Second Bite of the Cherry*? What's in it for me if I produce, for example, Lamb Baked in Orange for the family visit on Sunday, take Bran Muffins to work, have Fruity Muesli for breakfast and invite a friend to a lunch of Pasta with Broccoli and Pine Nuts?'

This is what's in it for you. You will better understand the **why, what** and **how** of good nutrition and appreciate the very substantial health benefits you can gain, *at any stage*, through new ways of thinking about food. As a result, you will be able to make **healthy** food choices the **easy** choices in your everyday life.

In this chapter we look at the fundamental idea that if we get our food right other parts of our lives will fall into place.

If you feel you have reached an impasse in your life and that you are locked in a pattern of living from which you'd like to break away, try changing what you eat along the lines presented in this book. You could discover that the changes bring a new zest for living from:

- good physical health — you're able to snap into the business of living from the time you wake up in the morning and with the drive to complete what you want to do each day.
- a way to be creative — like a potter with clay, you use food as a medium for self-expression to produce new taste, texture and colour combinations in the dishes you prepare.
- contact with people — you can use the cooking ideas in this book to make a get-together with friends an enjoyable and healthy experience.

Food Can be the Key to Open Doors to New Adventure

The starting point on this food adventure is to examine how we think about food.

The Meaning of Food in Different Contexts

We have to eat to live. What prompts us to eat? Part of the answer is that we have thoughts which guide our actions to eat. Lots of thoughts flash into our minds, such as 'I'm *hungry*', 'What will I have for dinner tonight?' and 'Should I have a second helping of that *delicious* pie?'

We also have thoughts which guide us to select particular foods. We tend to eat what we like — what we have good feelings about. These are the foods which have met our needs in the past and which we think of as tasty, easy to prepare or associated with good times. Does charcoal-grilled steak or chocolate cake come to mind?

Why do we choose to eat some foods and not others from the vast range available? The answer is that in different contexts particular foods have certain meanings for us as individuals. Take icecream for instance.

When we're young icecream has associations with parties, special treats and something tasty to eat in any given quantity. The belief that it could be a problem to our health doesn't enter our heads and we tuck-in with gusto.

When we have a family to feed, we may perceive icecream as a handy food to have in the freezer. It doesn't require any preparation, everybody likes it and it's an inexpensive treat. We're so busy with work and other activities that substituting home-made fruit salad or other nutritious desserts seldom happens. These dishes might take time to prepare and besides, the family might turn up their noses! Icecream is a safe option.

But icecream can take on a different meaning if we're watching our weight or our cholesterol. In this context, we might regard it with some caution and only eat it infrequently, because we now see it as a food laden with calories or fat.

This scenario is oversimplified and is not meant to put anyone off their favourite pudding! What we want to emphasise is that the meaning of a food (how we think about it in relation to ourselves), whether it be icecream or any other food, can vary according to context. This can apply to all sorts of experiences in our lives as illustrated by the statement of a woman who said 'When I was a girl one of my favourite stories was *Romeo and Juliet*. I read it over and over and I wept for Romeo and I wept for Juliet. Recently I read it again and I wept for their parents'. Our response is based not on the characteristics of objects and events but on how we see our personal relationship to them.

This leads to two important points. Firstly, not only do meanings change, **we can make them change** if we see an advantage in doing so. We can develop new thoughts about how enjoyable low-salt dishes are, for example, once we experiment with them. Have you tried to substitute other flavourings for salt in your casseroles? You will find that it's not difficult to develop a liking for low-salt alternatives, or low-fat foods for that matter, once you appreciate how important it is to do so for the sake of your long-term health.

Secondly, the time to act to impose new meanings on foods which will keep us healthy is in the middle years. The opportunity to protect the future, to eat more fibre and less fat, more beans and less cheese, mustn't be allowed to slip away. For at sixty we might have thirty more years in store and what

15

we do now could dramatically affect the quality of our lives in the years ahead.

Let's now examine why changing the way we think about food could be to our advantage.

Mum's Cooking Key to Unhealthy Diet

Dr William Castelli, head of the world's longest-running study of heart disease in Framingham, Massachusetts, thinks that the average person's lifetime diet is usually dictated by ten recipes — largely influenced by mum's cooking:

> Although the average person ate hundreds of different dishes in a lifetime, the general pattern of eating was restricted to the basic ten meals that the person likes to eat, knows how to cook and eats night after night. The recipes have usually been learned from what the parents ate.

He believes the key to changing a person's diet is often to change those ten habitual recipes. If this is done the risk of heart disease can be reduced considerably.

Thought for Food

We go to the supermarket or to our local shops, sometimes with a list of grocery items and sometimes without. And when we get home we find that we have chosen the usual staple items — some automatic purchases such as our breakfast cereal, eggs, milk, meat and packets of biscuits. If we're going to do some entertaining we will have some extra items. And there might be some indulgences. But usually our purchases are like those we have regularly made in the past. For the most part, the food we prepare and eat this week is very similar to last week's.

If we continually restrict ourselves to a very limited range of foods, and prepare them in the same old ways, we lose opportunities to be imaginative. More important perhaps, we run the risk of developing health problems if the old stand-by dishes we habitually use are high in fat and salt and low in fibre.

Why do we allow ourselves to develop such dull routines? Maybe we're in a bit of a rut and cut corners when it comes to food. Many of us have developed an efficient routine over the years of buying foodstuffs and cooking meals that requires the least possible effort. It takes time and thought, for instance, to forage through the fruit and vegetable stalls at a market or visit more than one greengrocer in search of freshly picked green beans or a piece of exotic fruit to garnish a salad.

Why should we make this extra effort or change our well-entrenched habits? We won't unless we can see some particular advantage to ourselves such as the important link between the food we eat and our health. In other words, we can only break out of a monotonous pattern of eating behaviour if we perceive that food can meet other needs in our lives apart from something to satisfy our appetites.

Unfortunately it's often only after the shock of a breakdown in health, such as the development of diabetes which requires very careful dietary management, that we start to think differently about food. Only then do we change what we eat. Wouldn't it be wise to take action before this happens if we want to continue to enjoy good health and the vital life that goes hand in hand with it? Mankind has thought about this for some time!

> Both in importance and in time, health precedes disease,
> so we ought to consider first how health may be preserved
> and then how one may best cure disease.
>
> Galen (AD 200)

What then is the precise role of food in preserving health once we're forty or over?

Food and Health

Good nutrition is critical if you are in the middle years and want to maintain, or regain, health for your long-term good.

Your food must provide an adequate supply of materials from which your body can extract what it requires for fuel, for the building and maintenance of tissues and for the regulation of its activities. You can't be healthy unless you eat foods which supply the substances which your body needs for proper

17

functioning. Again, you won't continue to enjoy health if you often eat foods which contain substances which are harmful, such as foods which are high in fat or salt.

The components in food which we need to keep healthy and the kinds of food which supply these components are discussed in Chapters 2 and 4.

It is worth considering just what is meant by the term 'health' before we go any further.

What is Health?

Montaigne, the famous sixteenth-century French philosopher said:

> Health is a precious thing ... the only thing indeed that deserves to be pursued at the expense not only of time, sweat, labour, worldly goods, but of life itself; since without health, pleasures, wisdom, knowledge, lose their colour and fade away. To my mind, no way that leads to health can be rugged, no means dearly bought.

In today's terms this precious thing called health is a state of high level well-being of body and mind in which we:

- get on with the business of living and do the things we want, unrestricted by constant lassitude or some malfunction of the heart, lungs or stomach, for example.
- bounce back after experiencing one of life's inevitable shocks, such as a bout of flu or a bereavement.
- adapt where necessary to changing circumstances, such as your partner's wish to start a new hobby or do more entertaining.

There are a number of implications, when we look at health in this way. For a start, it is **not**:

- merely the absence of disease. It is a positive state.
- a commodity dispensed by doctors. Modern medicine has certainly had its spectacular successes, but drugs and surgery can only bring limited relief when blood pressure is raised and arteries are clogged.
- related to age. It's possible to remain healthy until you're one hundred years old! The fact that you slow down as you get older doesn't mean you're unhealthy.
- enough to *talk* about the advantages and pleasures of good nutrition and physical exercise. In the final analysis, every

18

individual must take responsibility for preserving his or her own health and make appropriate efforts.

The Physical Signs of Good Health

- Good appetite
- Clear, bright eyes
- Quick recovery from minor illness
- Normal bowel function and regularity
- Healthy weight for height and age
- Ability to undertake some physical exercise

Your Health

Would you regard yourself as a healthy person in terms of these notions about health? You might like to ask yourself the questions, 'Am I as lively and as enterprising as I could be at my age? Could changing what I eat make me healthier and is it worth the effort?'

Read on to see what good nutrition can do to help you feel better now than you have done for years and to keep you healthy in the future.

The Dividends from Good Nutrition

Research on the nutritional needs of adults has produced clear evidence that, although good nutrition can't extend our life span, it can make our later years a time in which we keep doing the things we enjoy, feel glad to be alive and stay free of debilitating disease.

It makes good sense, then, to try to ensure that the period of healthy activity continues for as long as possible. Who would want a future filled with repeated severe infections, as can happen in diabetes, or with the paralysis which can follow a stroke?

There is, of course, a natural decline in our physical strength and powers of endurance as we get older. But good nutrition and regular exercise (see page 184), can considerably reduce the rate of decline and the likelihood of a breakdown in one or more of our body systems, such as the heart or kidneys. A comparison with the maintenance of a car helps to explain why this is so.

Principles of Good Maintenance

Our bodies are like cars. When they're new, problems seldom occur. There's no apparent harm done if the oil isn't changed periodically, if water full of sediment is used in the radiator or if the brakes and tyres aren't checked regularly.

What happens to a car as it gets older and hasn't been properly maintained? It keeps going until, suddenly, the crunch comes! At worst it careers off the road and crashes. If we're lucky it just won't start and the initial diagnosis of the breakdown service is failure of battery, starter motor and plugs. More detailed inspection at the garage reveals that the radiator is clogged with rust and that the engine is only running on three cylinders.

With our bodies, too, breakdowns in health can occur without warning. One day we're bowling along and the next we're flat on our backs in hospital crippled by illness. Or more commonly we start to 'misfire' and feel increasingly lethargic. Generally, we lose our zest for living and take more effort to get going in the morning.

Nutrition is essential for good maintenance. Therefore it's most important that the food we eat should contain the nutritional components which the body requires for easy starting and smooth running. It should not be loaded with substances which reduce the efficiency of the various organs, such as the heart, or which clog our arteries.

What Good Maintenance can Achieve:

- Reduced illness associated with heart disease, high blood pressure and diabetes.
- A healthy weight.
- Fewer problems with arthritis.
- Reduced rate of thinning of bones.
- Reduced susceptibility to, and quick recovery from, ailments such as colds and flu.
- Greater ability to undertake and enjoy some physical exercise.
- Normal bowel function and regularity.
- Reduced risk of illness and premature death from particular kinds of cancer such as of the colon and breast.

20

A sustained effort is required to keep healthy, which is the case with all proper maintenance. But — and this is worth bearing in mind — an investment of time, thought and effort is not the same as hardship, suffering and privation! You can keep yourself in fine fettle while you savour the exquisite texture of newly made wholemeal bread, the delicate succulence of Lamb Baked in Orange Juice and while you indulge your senses with the sight and smell of fresh fruits and vegetables in season.

It's Never Too Late

Don't ever accept the statement from anyone that you're too old to benefit from a change in your diet.

We have received some remarkable reports from people in their seventies and eighties who say how much they have enjoyed trying new high-fibre, low-fat dishes for example. Some of this group have also said that eating these foods has led to fewer problems with constipation. Others have mentioned that cutting out fried foods has reduced stomach pains.

These benefits from dietary change in later life are in accord with the findings of scientific studies. Some of this scientific evidence can be called 'hard' because there's a clear relationship between dietary change and improved health. Other scientific evidence can be called 'soft' or 'incomplete' because as yet it hasn't been possible to establish such direct relationships.

No matter what age you are, there is 'hard' evidence to indicate that following the dietary guidelines in this book can reduce potential or existing problems from such diseases as:

- Constipation and diverticulitis.
- Obesity.
- High blood cholesterol.
- High blood pressure.
- Diabetes.

There is growing, but still incomplete, evidence to suggest reduced risk of:

- Thrombosis.
- Diet-related cancer such as cancer of the colon.
- Periodontal (gum) disease.

There is no guarantee, of course, that improving the nutritional quality of your diet will make you healthy if you are already ill. Degenerative diseases such as diabetes and high blood pressure, which are linked at least in part to faulty nutrition earlier in life, take their toll and lead to breakdowns in body systems. The longer you have suffered from a disease condition the lower are your chances of markedly improving your health by changing your diet. Yet, at any age, there is the real possibility that you will start to feel more vital. It's always worth a go! No-one wants the unfortunate experience of Eubie Blake, the jazz pianist, who said plaintively on his hundredth birthday, 'If I had known I was going to live this long I would have taken better care of myself!'

Food and Creativity

If you are serious about improving the nutritional quality of your diet on a long term basis then it will require more than just replacing chips with boiled potatoes in the main course, or having yoghurt instead of a cream topping for dessert. Although these modifications are important to achieve a low-fat diet, they are mere tokens. What you must do to be effective is to rethink the whole meal, not just one or two of its parts.

This requires a careful review of all types of food activity from menu planning, shopping, food preparation, food presentation and (last but not least) eating. You may think this is a daunting prospect. Rest assured it isn't. It can be a highly creative experience. The ability to achieve 'one small triumph at a time' is the foundation of a life filled with 'profound satisfaction with the activities of daily life'. (René Dubos)

Some initial careful planning to do things differently and a little imagination in your daily life will pay handsome dividends in the health stakes. And what's more you'll have a lot of fun!

You might like to think about sharing these activities with

your partner if you don't already do so. One way could be to develop a system where you each take turns to purchase and prepare food on a week about basis, for instance.

This could be a creative pastime for men who have previously not regarded purchasing food and cooking as their responsibility. Why should they be deprived of this way to achieve a sense of fulfilment just because of an artificial barrier in their own minds about engaging in 'women's business'? There are many men who have sallied into the kitchen, at first tentatively and then with increasing confidence. Some of them have done so through force of circumstance, after becoming widowers, others by choice as a new hobby after retirement.

Let's do a breakdown of some of the main food activities to see how they can be a part of a more creative experience for now and the future than they might have been in the past.

Menu Planning

In the first place, there are important decisions to make about food — choices to promote health and pleasure for ourselves as well as perhaps for others. Planning a menu is a funny business in some ways. On the one hand, it's a way to create order in our lives. Once we've organised our day-to-day meals and purchased the foodstuffs for the next few days or week, we don't have to give any further thought to what we're going to eat. On the other hand, we can get into a rut if we plan our menus too rigidly without the breathing space to be spontaneous. Part of the creative experience is to act on a whim, such as prepare a dish we might have seen on a TV programme, or adjust or change a meal if unexpected visitors pop in.

You don't need to be locked into a pattern of preparing traditional breakfast, lunch and dinner dishes. Here's a new approach. The following novel menu ideas, some of which are based on the recipes in this book, demonstrate how you can experiment with a wide variety of food combinations which are deliciously different ... and **healthy**!

For breakfast — substitute cereal and toast with:
- Greek Rice with stewed apricots (see page 116).
- Currant Muffins (see page 112).
  or
- Minted Fruit Salad (see page 119).
- Wholemeal toast topped with asparagus and ricotta cheese.

or

- Tangy Apples (see page 126).
- Rye bread topped with smoked salmon.

or

- Toasted Muesli and Raspberries (see page 60).
- Wholemeal Pumpkin Scones (see page 127).

For lunch — instead of a sandwich, have:

- Cheesy Vegetables (see page 73).
- Fresh fruit

or

- Chicken Yoghurt Soup and Poppy Seed Turnovers (see pages 137 and 163).

or

- Cold cooked chicken with kiwi fruit slices, mango slices, purple grapes and sage leaf garnish.

or

- Canned salmon with fresh pineapple wedges, prunes, honeydew melon slices and tarragon garnish.

or

- Cottage or ricotta cheese with cherries, apple slices, melon slices and lemon balm garnish.

For dinner — substitute meat and three vegetables followed by icecream with:

- Savoury Pumpkin Pie and Cucumber Salad (see pages 100 and 75).
- Fruit Salad Soup (see page 63).

or

- Parsnip and Broccoli Soup and Moscow Piroshkis (see pages 65 and 120).
- Festive Fruit Basket (see page 113).

or

- Savoury Crêpes and Tabbouleh (see pages 130 and 79).
- Brandied Fruit and yoghurt (see page 110).

Shopping

Shopping can be an adventure in itself whether at the greengrocer for fruit and vegetables, the supermarket for groceries or speciality food shops for something exotic. Take time out to look for new fresh, canned or frozen foodstuffs.

Below is a check list of the basic food items to keep on hand so that you can create dishes based on the healthy diet guidelines in this book. These ingredients are:

- Cereal grains and flours
- Legumes (pulses)
- Pasta
- Nuts and seeds
- Dried fruits
- Canned unsalted vegetables
- Canned unsweetened fruit
- Fresh fruit and vegetables
- Frozen fruit and vegetables
- Polyunsaturated vegetable oil and margarine
- Low-fat milk, yoghurt and cheese
- Unsweetened fruit juice
- Herbs and spices
- Pickles, chutneys and mustard
- White and red wine
- Vinegar

Food Presentation

There is endless scope to make food look attractive and taste irresistible as well as be health promoting.

Eye appeal
Decorate food with one of the following garnishes:
- **Herbs** — chopped fresh herbs on soup, meat, fish and vegetables, a sprig of fresh mint on fruit salads and fruit drinks.
- **Fruit and vegetables** — cut into a variety of shapes — slices of citrus fruit on fish dishes or in fruit drinks, carrot curls or radish flowerettes on salads, unhulled strawberries on fruit soups.
- **Yoghurt** — a spoonful of yoghurt on chilled vegetable and fruit soups.
- **Spices** — saffron or paprika on savoury rice, nutmeg on creamed rice, chilli powder or paprika on cheese or yoghurt dips.

or

Serve food in dishes that complement one another in mood and colour. Use your favourite crockery, cutlery and glassware and enjoy it! A fresh flower, an attractive leaf, decorative ribbon or brightly coloured napkins or tablecloth can also add a touch of festivity to any dish. Here are some ideas to try — you may have many more. Use:
- White bowls for brightly coloured vegetables.
- Sparkling glassware for fresh fruit salads.
- Earthy, coloured pottery for hearty soups, casseroles and vegetarian dishes.

- Delicate china for decorative soufflés.
- Wooden platters for cheeses.
- Baskets for bread, rolls and nuts.

Taste appeal

- Use wine (from a cask) in casseroles.
- Pickles and chutneys complement the bland flavour of low-fat cheese.
- Spice, herb or fruit sauces can intensify the flavour of particular dishes.
- Add a tangy flavour to meat, poultry or fish dishes with citrus juice or rind.

Herbs in Cooking

Any mention of ways to boost the taste of food would not be complete without some reference to herbs. They are particularly important in low-fat and low-salt dishes. A tub of fresh herbs in a sunny spot in the garden and a rack of dried herbs and spices in the kitchen are essential culinary tools. Fresh herbs are a delicious sandwich-filler, mixed with cheese, cold meat or salads.

Parsley and **Mint** are probably the most widely used herbs in garnishing salads, sauces and soups. However, there are many other herbs which can be used in cooking, each with their own unique flavour.

- **Basil**: Has a spicy aroma — use in tomato sauces for pasta dishes.
- **Chives**: Have a mild onion flavour — use in low-fat cheese dishes, soups, sauces.
- **Coriander (Chinese parsley):** Has a strong lemon flavour — use in curries.
- **Dill:** Has an aniseed flavour — good with seafood dishes.
- **Marjoram:** Is closely related to oregano in flavour — use in casseroles, tomato sauces.
- **Oregano:** Has a pungent flavour and is used in many Mediterranean dishes — spaghetti sauces, pizzas and salads.
- **Rosemary:** Has a very strong flavour — use in lamb and pork dishes.
- **Sage:** Another strong flavour — use in stuffing for meat and poultry.

- **Thyme:** There are different varieties and flavours — use in tomato dishes, casseroles, stuffing for meat and poultry.

Food Preparation

The **kitchen**, which is where most of our food preparation takes place, must be both attractive and functional. You don't necessarily need to pull out cupboards, replace the old stove with a built-in oven and microwave and buy a new matching refrigerator and freezer set! Here are a few ideas which will cost much less yet make the most important room in the house a pleasant and functional environment in which to work.

Cooking utensils:
- A good set of sharp knives to trim fat off meat and prepare vegetables and salads.
- A pair of sharp, strong scissors to trim fat off bacon and chicken, the fins off fish and to cut up herbs.
- Chopping boards in various sizes.
- Food processor.
- Stainless steel saucepans for quick cooking and easy cleaning.
- Assorted mixing bowls, casserole and serving dishes.
- Wooden spoons, beaters and strainers.
- A non-stick frying pan is a good investment.

Useful storage and decorative items:
- A notice board for news clippings, recipe and menu ideas and last but not least, a copy of the Healthy Diet Triangle. (Opposite page 33.)
- Open shelves for jars of food items used regularly.
- Terracotta pot or window box for fresh herbs.
- Hanging baskets to store vegetables and fruit.
- Bread baskets on wall hooks for easy storage.
- Recipe books displayed prominently for easy access.
- Colourful food posters, prints and photos to brighten up walls.
- A couple of chairs or stools to sit on while preparing food or for when friends pop in for coffee.

As you can see, a healthy eating regime is based to a large extent on how creative we are in choosing and preparing the food we eat. These activities go well beyond being a necessary part of our daily lives. They could help to prevent the development of the unfortunate condition known as **rustout**.

Avoiding Rustout

It has been said that 'When a person retires from life, life retires from the person'.

General practitioners have observed that many people, particularly men, are in good health when they retire from work. However, they quickly develop symptoms of illness after completing routine tasks around the home or travelling around the country or overseas. This condition is called **rustout**. It is due to inadequate care of oneself. When we are bored, fatigued, frustrated or dissatisfied following a period of understimulation we tend to neglect our bodies and become ill.

Food — how we think about it and what we do with it — is a crucial factor in determining whether or not we develop rustout. If we continue to eat the same old foods prepared in the same old ways we'll be right on track for this condition. It can be avoided however, if we recognise that being creative with food not only helps to keep us healthy but is mentally stimulating. Here's how to avoid rustout.

- **Put into practice** the kind of ideas outlined in the section on Food and Creativity (page 22).
- **Take risks** — be bold and extend your culinary skills to produce dishes which are just right. Stretching for success will keep you on your toes.
- **Keep up to date** — it's been well said that a person should be part of the action of his or her times. Keep a look out for new fresh and processed foodstuffs. You'll be amazed how many interesting products there are to try if you set out to look for them. You might discover a new type of vegetable at the greengrocer, or a bean sauce that you can really enjoy in an Asian delicatessen.
- **Keep in contact** —use food to keep lines of communication open with those who are important to you and to overcome feelings of being disconnected from others. Inviting relatives or friends to share a new dish can be a way to create an interesting and enjoyable experience for all as well as a way to rekindle special bonds.

Overcoming Barriers to Change

The joy of living is confronting a problem and solving it.

Even though we may be determined to modify our eating pattern we often find it difficult to do so. Why is this? A useful explanation is that we have thoughts which guide our feelings and actions based on the meanings we personally impose on particular foods.

Our thoughts may be barriers to change. Let's examine the notion, for example, that a particular food is thought of as a 'treat'. This helps to explain why a pattern of eating develops from which it may be difficult to break away.

One woman, who had serious weight problems, told us that eating sugary desserts each day met her need for a real treat. She could not escape from this pattern of eating because she said there was little else in her life which gave her such a feeling of pleasure.

The association in her mind between a dessert and a treat was formed during her childhood, as her own story shows:

> As a child of the depression years my mother's main aim was to fill us up. We ate economical dishes like stew with dumplings or steamed jam roly-poly, a dough-like substance which stuck to your ribs like glue.
>
> To leave anything on your plate was considered either bad manners or evil. You ate everything that was put in front of you. Any leftovers were kept to use again or we were kidded to 'eat it to save it' or made to feel guilty that 'the poor people of China would be glad to eat it'. Waste not, want not — that was the extent of the food message.
>
> Nutrition was an unknown word. If we were good we were rewarded with an icecream or a lolly, and desserts were the treat which came after — if you ate all your dinner and vegies you could have some jelly or whatever. Mum's 'stick-jaw toffee' was a real treat. It actually did stick one's jaws (whatever did it do to teeth?).

As we can see, while she continued to perceive that she needed the gratification provided by sweet treats, she would find it difficult to adopt a healthy pattern of eating and lose weight.

Does this personal reminiscence ring a bell? Was food linked to reward or punishment in your childhood? The anecdote certainly conveys very graphically a sense of the powerful feelings developed about food which arose from a particular set of experiences in childhood. We can empathise with the young girl's need for 'a real treat'. Don't we all have periodic cravings for our favourite soft-centred chocolates or Danish pastries?

There are a host of other reasons, besides wanting a treat, which help explain why we continue to eat foods in which we wouldn't indulge if we felt more in control of our lives. For instance, there is the need to be part of a group — so we eat similar foods to other group members — and the enjoyment of particular taste sensations, such as a sharp-flavoured cheese or a smooth-textured dessert, without which we might think life rather dreary.

We don't have to be locked in to a pattern of eating these foods every day, just because we enjoy them. There is a way to escape from such an unhealthy syndrome.

This is to create new meanings about food through following some of the suggestions in this chapter. The oral gratification of sweet desserts and fatty cheeses will then be more than offset by the sense of pleasure and achievement we obtain from doing things with food that keep us stimulated and healthy. Grilled Savoury Fish and Minted Fruit Salad will fit the bill nicely, thank you!

Food and Socialising

In the previous section we focused primarily on what we can do with health-promoting food to make it appealing. Here we look at the advantages of using this type of food in the way we relate to others, which includes making new friends.

What do you value most as you get older? Among the possible answers, such as financial security, a comfortable home and treasured possessions, there is one which appears at the top of many people's list — good friends. We humans are social creatures. We need company, even if it's only one person, and we generally experience a sense of contentment when surrounded by our friends.

From time immemorial, food has always played a prominent role at social gatherings whether they be birthday celebrations, house-warmings or casual get-togethers with friends. Sharing food is closely linked to expressions of personal acceptance, friendliness and warmth.

One of the problems many people face who suffer from such diet-related problems as obesity or high blood pressure is that a social function can become an ordeal instead of something to look forward to as a pleasurable occasion. The **type** of food served is the problem. Should they eat the rich calorie-laden food that is placed before them and suffer the health consequences or should they avoid it and feel a sense of deprivation? Neither choice is an attractive proposition!

Many of us are conditioned to think that food should be a culinary indulgence at a social gathering. Predictably, it is often cooked in a great deal of fat or salt or decorated with lashings of cream. There is often little or no attention paid to whether it is wholesome. This is because when we prepare food for a social occasion, we tend to limit our questions to 'Does it taste good and look good?' rather than 'Will it have taste, eye *and* health appeal for my guests?'

You could not be blamed for thinking, 'It's one thing for me to become more health-orientated when choosing and cooking the foods I eat on my own. It's quite another matter when it comes to hosting friends, relatives, neighbours, business acquaintances or whoever else I may be entertaining. They might not like these so called healthy meals and furthermore they may be put-off by something so different from a conventional meal.'

Our answer to these perfectly reasonable fears is that your relatives, friends or casual acquaintances are very likely to love you for it. They will feel that they have eaten well and adventurously. For instance, if you produced a wholemeal banana cake for a birthday treat instead of a chocolate cream sponge, you may be pleasantly surprised by the response. There could be sighs of relief all round as your guests are faced with the refreshing prospect of eating something light and healthy instead of another indulgence. And what's more it can look just as decorative as a gâteau. Topped with toasted sesame seeds and walnut halves with a brightly coloured ribbon around its diameter, the banana cake could grace any table.

What we're advocating in this book is that you can have your cake and eat it too — so to speak! If you use the Healthy Diet Triangle as the basis for creating your own meals and the recipes in Chapter 3, you can produce any number of dishes at a social function which will be both delicious and nutritious.

Making New Friends

There are times in our lives when we feel the need to take steps to get to know more people and make new friends. This may happen when we move to a different part of town or the country, when the last of our children leave home or when we retire from our job. Whatever the reason for wanting to make contact with new people — it's a healthy sign. Those who retain their vitality are the 'lucky people who need people' — and who do something about it.

Use food as a way to get to know a person you would like as a friend. Invite him or her to your home and make something a bit different — Veal Stuffed Courgettes (see page 158) followed by Apricot Wine Soup (see page 61). There's the distinct possibility that you would introduce a lively element into the conversation, which is a good start to a friendship.

If it's a group of people you want to get to know, such as new neighbours, new colleagues or members of a club you have recently joined, do something similar. Producing a healthy and pleasing meal could be the step to enlarging the circle of people whose company could enrich your life — and vice versa.

Summary

A new style of healthy eating can be the way to achieve a successful second go at life — a second bite of the cherry! Once we appreciate that food can be the means to a more vital life in the future we can start to develop a new approach to the food we prepare and eat.

As we have pointed out in this chapter, there are substantial advantages which flow on from different ways of thinking about food — the main one being better health. But what we also want to emphasise is, that if you continue to see that life's simple delights come from sweet desserts or cheese sauces, eat them every now and then and don't lead the life of a miser.

This chapter has focused on **why** the food we eat is so critical to good health and to a sense of being in more control of our lives and our futures. Chapter 2 takes this a step further and outlines **what** to eat to achieve these goals.

The Healthy Diet Triangle

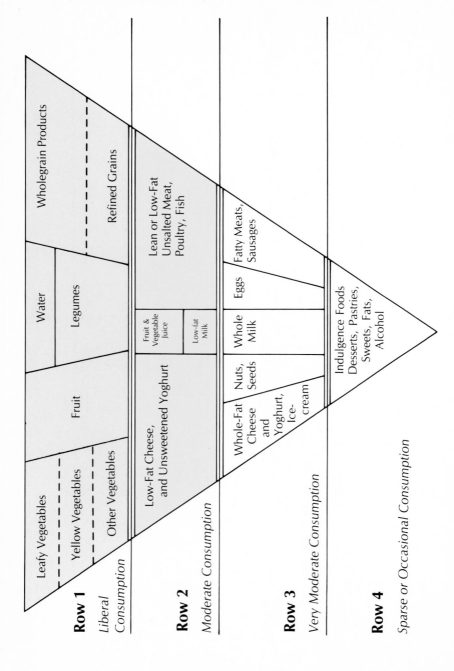

2
The Healthy Diet Triangle

Introduction

The **Healthy Diet Triangle**, shown opposite, is a modern, scientific guide of what to eat for health — and pleasure. You could find it very helpful for answering the basic question:

How can I develop a dietary pattern which has foods which I like and which, at the same time, will keep me healthy and allow me to take advantage of what modern technology offers?

The answer is to make **healthy** choices **easy** choices for yourself.

This is easier said than done of course! However, a creative approach to food is part of the process, as we discussed in the previous chapter. Access to recipes for marvellous new dishes made from grains, beans, fruits and vegetables, such as those in the next chapter, is another part of the process. Here we look at which foods are 'healthy choices' and which should be the mainstay of our everyday fare.

The Triangle is a powerful and easy-to-follow guide to healthy food choices and has substantial scientific backing. It represents what we want to emphasise throughout this book. Healthy eating arises from variety and moderation in food

33

choices, not from a series of prescriptions on 'eat this but don't eat that'. Let's look briefly at the origins of the Triangle and then examine how it can be used to make daily food choice decisions.

The Need for the Healthy Diet Triangle

Every day we are faced with more and more choices to make when we look at the increasing number of products in the supermarket and other food outlets. At the same time we are bombarded with media messages about the 'natural goodness' of one food and the 'preservative-free' value of another.

These parallel developments have been accompanied by controversy over such issues as what 'natural goodness' and 'chemical additives' really mean. This has led to a great deal of scaremongering. No wonder shoppers can be heard to apologise for their purchases, muttering shamefacedly 'I know it's bad for me', to be comforted by the stock response, 'So is everything, nowadays!' How can we get on with healthy living if we think that virtually anything we eat or drink is likely to be unhealthy and that all pleasures are illegal, immoral or cause cancer in mice!

A number of authoritative scientific councils have set out, in the past few years, to provide positive guidance and dispel this pessimistic view so that we can be confident about our food choices. The aim of these councils is to focus attention on food rather than dietary supplements as the source of good nutrition.

Dietary Guidelines

Dietary guidelines have been drawn up to provide a framework on which people can make choices about what to eat for long term health:

1. Promote breast feeding.
2. Choose a nutritious diet from a variety of foods.
3. Control your weight.
4. Avoid eating too much fat.

34

5. Avoid eating too much sugar.
6. Eat more breads and cereals (preferably wholegrain) and vegetables and fruits.
7. Limit alcohol consumption.
8. Use less salt.

The Healthy Diet Triangle is a way of presenting similar ideas in an easily understandable, diagrammatic form.

The 'Big Three' Dietary Guidelines

The three main points to keep constantly in mind for proper maintenance of your body are:

- **Fibre**
  If you increase fibre in your diet you will achieve the benefits that fibrous materials bring and you will automatically increase intakes of complex carbohydrates, vitamins and minerals.
- **Fat**
  If you adapt to a lower-fat diet you will find it a lot easier to control your weight and you will reduce your chances of suffering from a number of degenerative diseases.
- **Variety**
  If you consistently add variety to your diet you will increase your chances of being well nourished.

Principles on Which the Healthy Diet Triangle has been Constructed

A wealth of scientific knowledge about food and nutrition has been presented in this form to show that healthy eating in the 1980s:

- is a matter of frequency. There's a place for all foods, including our favourite indulgences, but we do ourselves a service if we eat some foods more frequently than others.
- is based on eating more of foods in the top two rows.
- comes from choosing a wide variety of foods. There is a great deal of scope for alternative food choices within the guidelines incorporated in the Triangle.

- can include foods which are either fresh or processed. Pre-cooked breakfast cereals and canned tuna, for example, have a role in a dietary pattern which underlies good health, as do fresh and frozen vegetables and fish.
- can be achieved by attention to a small number of nutritional factors. This simplifies the decisions to be made about whether a particular food or combination of foods should have a place in our diet.

The Content of the Healthy Diet Triangle

We'll examine each row in turn, listing the nutritional components found in the foods, and then discuss their significance.

We should focus on **Row 1** and **Row 2** foods because they are the ones which will provide all the nutritional components our bodies need for healthy functioning. The foods in the bottom two rows are less concentrated sources of these components and are also higher in substances which could do us harm, mainly fat and salt.

- **Row 1** foods provide us with starch (the best fuel for our bodies), protein (particularly from legumes), all the vitamins except B12, many mineral elements and all our dietary fibre.
- **Row 2** foods supply protein and are the main sources of calcium (milk and other dairy products apart from butter) and iron (meat and fish). The critical feature of Row 2 foods is that they are low in fat.
- **Row 3** foods also contribute valuable nutritional components. However they are generally high in fat and salt and therefore should be eaten in moderation.
- **Row 4** foods are those that we tend to associate with indulgences or treats. In short, they are what our children might describe as 'yummy' (apart from alcohol!). They are low in essential nutrients and should only be eaten occasionally.

The Key Nutritional Components

There are thousands of substances in food. Most of them, such as those which contribute to flavour, are not essential to the proper functioning of our bodies. For example there are over 70 substances which add to the flavour of tea. They do not perform any nutritional function, nor do us any harm.

Nutritional components are the substances which our bodies need from food (the essential nutrients), or which are common ingredients of foods which harm us if eaten in excess, such as salt. The scientific study of foods has shown that there are **five** main classes of nutritional components which affect the maintenance of good health. These are:

1. Sources of energy or fuel
2. Nutrients — mainly proteins, vitamins and minerals
3. Water
4. Dietary fibre
5. Substances which may have harmful effects if eaten in excess

A balanced diet from a wide variety of foods provides enough energy, nutrients, water and fibre and is low in potentially harmful substances. Constructing a balanced diet would be a full time occupation if we had to check that we were getting enough nutrients each day. For there are about 50 of these, which include essential amino acids, vitamins and minerals.

In practice there are only a small number of nutritional components we need to think about when developing a healthy pattern of eating. These are:

- Dietary fibre
- Dietary fat
- Calcium
- Salt

If the quantities eaten of these components are right, not too little and not too much, then it is highly likely that the intake of other components will be right too. This means that we don't have to worry about protein, vitamins and minerals, apart from calcium.

In this chapter we look at why dietary fibre and fat are critical nutritional components. The others on the list are discussed in Chapter 4.

But first we need to examine a few more features of the Healthy Diet Triangle.

Selecting Fresh and Packaged Foods

There is an ever-widening range of foods available which fall into the top two rows of the Triangle.

Look at the variety of vegetables that are available today, for instance. Ten years ago you could only purchase one or two types of lettuce. Now there are a number of different types on the market. You can see this dramatic change for yourself when you look along the shelves of your greengrocer.

Processed foods are also included in the top two rows. Frozen vegetables come immediately to mind, as do breads and breakfast cereals. Again, the range of packaged foods which can be classified as 'nutritious' and 'good for me' is growing rapidly as food manufacturers respond to consumer demands for products which, for example, are low in fat and salt, and high in fibre.

It's worth thinking about including some of these processed foodstuffs in your diet because of what they offer in variety, ease of preparation and storage, in addition to being nutritious. Chapter 4 discusses how you as the consumer can be 'nutrition-wise' in the supermarket.

The Healthy Diet Triangle and 'Favourite' Foods

You may have a sense of deprivation when you look at the Triangle for the first time. It's all very well to modify eating patterns for health reasons but what about favourite items such as the skin of a roast chicken or home-made cheesecake which would both be classified as **Row 3** and **Row 4** foods?

The answer is that foods which you are particularly fond of can certainly have a place in your diet. The Triangle doesn't indicate that Row 3 and 4 foods are off-limits, only that they should have a relatively small place in your diet. Is that so hard to put into practice?

The Healthy Diet Triangle and your Food Budget

The cost of food is not related to its nutritional value. Some of the best sources of good nutrition are inexpensive staples such as cereals, potatoes, legumes and vegetables and fruit in season.

There are many tasty recipes (see Chapter 3) which are made up of ingredients that are both nutritious and cheap. And there are many meals that can be made from Row 1 and Row 2 foods which don't need much cooking either. A healthy diet is based, to a very large extent, on the care taken to combine colour, texture and taste of everyday staples to enchant the palate.

The Main Contributors to Healthy Eating

Row 1 foods:
- Vegetables, fruits
- Legumes (beans and lentils)
- Cereal grain products (rice, pasta, wholemeal bread)

Do you think you'll suffer any hardship from *increasing* these foods in your daily fare? One glance at the Row 1 recipes in Chapter 3 should dispel any possible fear of this.

Row 2 foods:
- Low-fat dairy products (ricotta cheese, cottage cheese, yoghurt, milk)
- Lean meat (rump steak, topside mince, veal fillets)
- Fish and poultry (fat-trimmed)

These are the foods which should be used like **condiments** with Row 1 foods, as far as possible. For example, brown fried rice can be regarded as the main meal item on your dinner plate, with a savoury topping of sautéd beef as the condiment.

Recommended Daily Intakes for Adults

Row 1 Foods				
Vegetables	Fruits	Wholegrain cereals *or*	Wholemeal breads *or*	Rice Pasta
2-6 serves, at least one raw	2-4 pieces, at least one citrus	115 g (4 oz)	2-4 slices	340-450 g (12-16 oz)

Row 2 Foods			
Lean meat, fish, poultry *or*	Legumes (from Row 1)	Low fat milk or yoghurt *or*	Cheese
1-2 serves 100-200 g (3-6 oz)	170-200 g (5-6 oz)	600 ml (1 pt)	45 g (1½ oz)

Menu Example

Here is an example of a day's menu which is in accord with the guidelines in the Healthy Diet Triangle:

Breakfast:
- Juice of one orange
- 60 g (2 oz) muesli, 125 ml (¼ pt) milk
- 1 slice wholemeal toast lightly spread with peanut butter

Lunch:
- sandwiches
  2 slices wholemeal bread, lightly buttered
  bean sprouts
  20 g (¾ oz) ricotta cheese
  tomato slices
- apple

Dinner:
- Baked Paprika Fish — 1 fillet (See page 141.)
- 2 new potatoes steamed in jackets
- large serve of tossed vegetable salad
- 1 serve stewed fruit with 1 cup low-fat yoghurt

Throughout day:
- Tea, coffee with extra milk
- Fresh fruit, 1 to 3 pieces
- Scone or muffin, lightly buttered

Dietary Fibre

Dietary fibre is indigestible material in plant food. It is a mixture of plant cell wall material, such as cellulose and lignin — which produce the hardness of leaves and stalks — and soluble materials such as pectins, which help the setting process in jam and gums. Today fibre should be regarded as more than roughage because of the recognition of the importance of these soluble substances.

Virtually all fruits and vegetables contain significant amounts of soluble fibre. However, the richest sources of soluble fibre are legumes, for example, red kidney beans, baked beans, dried peas and lentils. Other good sources of soluble fibre are oats, barley or rye — porridge, pearl barley in soups, rye bread.

Action to take:
Choose foods for their fibre content.

- The **Fibre Counter** shows which foods are particularly useful sources of fibre in the diet.
- Aim to get about 30 g (a little more than 1 oz) or more of fibre each day. Breakfast is a good opportunity to boost fibre intake.
- Don't equate fibre with bran and bran-containing foods. The fibre in vegetables is probably of more value than bran.
- Boost your intake of fluids.

Significance of Fibre in the Diet

There are several reasons why fibre is important:

- It adds bulk because it holds water and helps to keep the bowels working smoothly. The main increase in bulk is due to the growth of harmless bacteria that live in the gut and can use fibre as food. The gas, which is also produced as part of this process, also makes the contents softer and more bulky. This all helps to promote regular and easy bowel actions and reduces unnecessary straining.

  When you increase the amount of fibre in your diet you can experience the health benefits quickly because your digestive system can begin to work better within days.

- Soluble fibres have been found to lower blood cholesterol and to modify carbohydrate absorption so as to improve glucose tolerance. This is of particular significance to diabetics.

- It has the ability to bind toxins and carcinogens (cancer-producing substances). These undesirable substances are eliminated more quickly from the bowel because bulky fibrous material serves to dilute them and produces more frequent bowel actions.

  The fibrous, bulky food eaten by people in rural Africa, for example, may be a contributing factor to the low prevalence in such communities of bowel disorders such as diverticular disease, hiatus hernia, haemorrhoids, irritable bowel and cancer of the colon.

- Foods high in fibre tend to be more chewy and more filling than their low-fibre counterparts. For these reasons foods such as wholemeal bread are useful for weight control.

- Foods which contribute fibre to the diet also provide starch, protein, vitamins and minerals.

If you select foods which provide sufficient fibre (20 to 30 grams or ⅔ to 1 ounce or more per day) you will automatically ensure that you are taking in adequate quantities of most of the nutritional components that your body needs for healthy functioning.

The proviso is that no more than a third of this should come from bran. Most should come from the foods which contain soluble fibre.

Which Foods Contain Fibre?

Fibre is found in Row 1 foods. Some of these also contain starch and/or protein such as grain products and legumes, while others contain vitamins and minerals such as fruit and vegetables.

Foods which contain both fibre and starch are the best sources of fuel we can choose. These are potatoes, rice, pasta, bananas, beans, peas, porridge, breakfast cereals which contain bran and wholemeal breads, rolls and scones. (See Complex Carbohydrates, page 172.)

Fibre Counter

Check how much fibre you have each day

	SERVE SIZE	FIBRE (grams)	YOUR DAY'S FOOD	
			No. of serves	Total grams
CEREALS				
Allbran	60 g (2 oz)	9		
bran (unprocessed)	2 tblsp	6		
muesli	60 g (2 oz)	8		
porridge (cooked)	150 g (5 oz)	3		
Rice crispies	30 g (1 oz)	1		
Corn flakes	30 g (1 oz)	1		
Special K	30 g (1 oz)	0.5		
Weetabix	2 biscuits (30 g)	4		
rice — brown (cooked)	115 g (4 oz)	3		
— white (cooked)	115 g (4 oz)	1		
pasta — white (cooked)	115 g (4 oz)	3		
— wholemeal (cooked)	115 g (4 oz)	6		
BREAD				
wholemeal (high fibre)	1 slice	3		

(continued next page)

Fibre Counter (*continued*)

	SERVE SIZE	FIBRE (grams)	YOUR DAY'S FOOD	
			No. of serves	Total grams
wholemeal	1 slice	2		
Vogel	1 slice	2		
multigrain	1 slice	2		
white (high fibre), brown	1 slice	1.5		
rye	1 slice	1.5		
white	1 slice	1		
BISCUITS				
Ryvita	1	1		
Vitawheat	1	1		
sweet biscuits with nuts/fruit	1	1		
CAKES				
plain doughnut, yeast bun	1	0		
fruit cake	1 slice	1–2		
FRUIT				
apple, pear	1	3		
apricots	4	3		
banana	1	3		
orange, peach	1	2		
plums	3–4	2		
pineapple	1 slice	1		
sultanas, dates, raisins	25 g (1 oz)	2		
tomato	1	1		
fruit juices		0		

(*continued next page*)

Fibre Counter (*continued*)

	SERVE SIZE	FIBRE (grams)	YOUR DAY'S FOOD	
			No. of serves	Total grams
VEGETABLES				
beans — French or string	115 g (4 oz)	2		
broad, baked	115 g (4 oz)	6		
broccoli	115 g (4 oz)	2		
cabbage, corn	115 g (4 oz)	2		
spinach	115 g (4 oz)	2		
carrots	115 g (4 oz)	2		
cauliflower	115 g (4 oz)	1		
pumpkin	115 g (4 oz)	1		
zucchini	115 g (4 oz)	1		
peas	115 g (4 oz)	3		
potato (peeled)	1	1		
(with skin)	1	3		
NUTS				
peanuts	30	2		
almonds	13	2		
ANIMAL PRODUCTS meat, fish, poultry, and dairy products do not contain fibre				
YOUR TOTAL FIBRE FOR THE DAY:				

Our thanks go to Mrs Gwen Wilkinson, Senior Dietitian at Modbury Hospital, Adelaide, for supplying the information in this counter.

How Much Fibre?

The two main ways to establish whether you are taking in enough fibre are:

- Easy passage of stools. You appreciate that what is known as 'roughage' is better named 'softage' or 'smoothage'.

45

- Stools are bulky and usually float. You classify yourself as a floater rather than a sinker!

To achieve these ends you should aim for at least 25 grams of fibre per day. You can use the Fibre Counter to find out how close you are to this figure.

But don't go overboard with bran! If you do you might experience discomfort as your gut tries to adapt to the unaccustomed material. You'll experience minimal problems if your increased fibre comes from eating. a little more each of vegetables, legumes, salads, fruit and cereal foods.

What About Fibre Supplements?

These may be of short-term value in relieving constipation in circumstances such as illness. Their long-term effects are not known. Fibre supplements should not be used as an alternative to increased intake of fibre from a combination of Row 1 foods. The particular fibre they contain could not bring the same benefits as the whole range of fibrous materials found in cereals, fruits, vegetables and legumes.

Advertisements for fibre supplements suggest that it's difficult to get enough dietary fibre from foods. This is not true, as you'll quickly discover for yourself when you try some of the Row 1 recipes in this book.

Fat

Action to take:
Reduce the amount of all types of fat in your daily diet.

- Find out which foods are the main sources of fat in your diet and try various means to reduce your frequency of consumption of these foods.
- Identify and avoid foods which contain hidden fat.
- Reduce the amount of fat you add to food in cooking and serving. (See Cooking Methods, page 176.)
- Be a trimmer if you want to be trimmer.

Why pick on Fat?

Fat is more responsible for the clogging of arteries and the development of overweight than any other component in food. Even if you don't become a victim of heart disease, the effects of overweight can lead to breathlessness and aching joints. Who wants to face the future in that condition?

Fat is extremely energy-dense. (See Energy Considerations, page 182.) Weight gain is more likely to occur when you eat food with a high energy density. For example, if you consistently took in 400 kilojoules per day more than you used — the amount of dietary energy in 30 g (1 oz) of cheddar cheese — you would put on 5 kg (11 lb) of fat in a year.

Someone recently told us how she lost a substantial amount of weight when she reduced the fat in her diet. She said, 'I hadn't realised how many kilojoules there were in fat and how many foods were high in fat. I found it much easier to lose weight once I started to focus on where fat was coming from in my diet, particularly from cheese.'

You will be surprised at how much better you feel if you substantially reduce the amount of fat in your diet. Here is the experience of someone who did this. 'I used to wake up at about three in the morning with stomach pains. They disappeared after I replaced part of the meat in my dinner with extra vegetables.'

Obvious and Hidden Fats

One of the problems with reducing fat intake is that it is not always easy to detect. For a start it does not have as characteristic a taste as sugar. Secondly, although fat can be easily seen in some foods such as chops and bacon, and in the oil you use in cooking, it is difficult to detect in others. You can't see the fat in cheese, peanuts and avocados for example.

Some authorities divide the fat we eat into two categories: 'visible' and 'invisible'. A more useful system is to divide fats into 'obvious' and 'hidden' using the eye test.

If you can see it it's obvious, if you can't it's hidden. Of all the fat we eat, about half falls into each category.

Much of the obvious fat we eat comes from meat, oils used in cooking and salad dressings. Significant sources of hidden fats are cheese, pastries, chocolate and ice cream.

Where to Start with Fat Reduction

Decide that you will limit high-fat foods to one meal per day if you are accustomed to eating such foods. For example, if you usually have a roast or chops for your evening meal then you should only eat low-fat meals at other times of the day. Substitute muesli for egg and bacon at breakfast, a salad roll for a cheese roll for lunch, fruit for cheese as snacks.

The Next Stage

Once you've made the start suggested above try some of the Row 2 recipes in Chapter 3. You could be surprised at just how pleasurable are, for example, the delicate and subtle flavours of Spiced Chicken Wings, and Lamb Baked in Orange.

Other Strategies to Reduce Fat Intake

Here are some ideas on how to cut down on the quantity you eat of fatty foods.
- Try more vegetable-based dishes. Use boiled or baked potatoes, rice, beans, peas or lentils as the base, with perhaps a little meat for flavour. That way you get less fat and more fibre.
- Eat fish instead of meat. It has less fat and some possible extra health promoting properties. (See Fish, page 186.)

Cholesterol

The story of cholesterol and its relationship to saturated fats and risk factors for coronary heart disease is too well known to repeat here. Up-to-date information on cholesterol can be obtained by contacting the nearest office of the National Heart Foundation.

There is still no agreement among nutritional authorities on whether we should substitute polyunsaturated fats (oils and margarines labelled as such) for saturated fats — solid, mainly animal (including dairy) fats.

Use polyunsaturated oils and spreads if you have high blood lipids.

We have nominated the use of polyunsaturated fats in the recipes. The amount of these in the recipes is limited, in accord with the guideline on which there is much more agreement — to reduce the total amount of fat eaten.

Red Meat

Most of the fat we eat comes from red meats. There is plenty of scope for reducing the intake of fat from this source without reducing the consumption and enjoyment of lean beef, lamb or pork. For example:

- Trim outside fat from meat before cooking. (Be trimmer through being a trimmer is worth bearing in mind.)
- Buy lean cuts of meat and lean mince — the extra cost can be offset by having smaller serving sizes.
- Limit the serving size of meat and eat more vegetables or salads at main meals.
- Choose cooking methods which do not use added fat, such as grilling, baking, dry-frying and stewing. (See Cooking Methods, page 176.)
- Use a rack when grilling, roasting or baking meats to remove fat.
- Make gravy for roast meat with meat juices only — remove all fat first.
- Skim fat off casseroles and stews.
- Try experimenting with meat as a condiment, as in Asian-style cooking, rather than as the centrepiece of a meal.
- Buy sausages from a butcher who you know uses lean meat.
- Eat less processed and tinned meats.

Note: Be a trimmer with chicken too when preparing a casserole.

Cheese

The intake of high-fat cheeses also need to be carefully watched. It's very difficult to see how much fat is in cheese. Just try grilling cheddar cheese and see how much fat oozes out!

49

CHEESE	FAT CONTENT (g per 100 g)
Cottage cheese	4
Ricotta	14
Cheese spread	23
Edam-type	23
Camembert-type	23
Processed cheese	25
Danish Blue-type	29
Cheddar-type	34
Cream cheese	47

If you think that life would be very dreary without your cheese here are some ideas:
- Choose better-quality mature cheeses — these are stronger, have a better flavour and less is required in cooking.
- Use stronger cheese for cheese sauces, as less is required for flavour.
- When eating cheese with bread, try omitting the butter as Mediterranean people do — it's much healthier.
- Try low-fat cheeses such as cottage and ricotta in place of the cheeses you would normally eat for example with Welsh rarebit, soufflés and other savoury dishes.
- Use pickles or chutneys with low-fat cheeses on toast or biscuits.

Note: If you haven't done so already, you should switch to low-fat (1.5 per cent fat) milk. This contains half the fat of ordinary milk and tastes almost the same.

Other Sources of Fat

Foods which should be eaten sparingly, particularly when you have already had **meat** or **cheese** that day:
- Chocolate
- Peanut butter
- Tuna with oil
- Icecream
- Nuts — walnuts, cashews, almonds, peanuts
- Avocados
- Eggs
- Pastries — pies, sausage rolls

Added Fats and Oils

What we add to food, either as solids (fat) or liquids (oils) is another major source of fat. There is no difference in their energy (37 kilojoules or 9 calories per gram) contents.

Here are some ideas for reducing the amount of added fats and oils in the food you eat:

- Do not add fat to cooked food, for example, cream to soups and desserts, butter to vegetables (a *little* butter or margarine on boiled potatoes is acceptable). Don't serve fatty sauces on meat.
- Try low-fat salad dressings.
- Use butter or margarine sparingly on bread (thick slices), toast, rolls, biscuits, crumpets, muffins and buns.
- Choose cooking methods for fish, chicken and meat which do not use added fat, such as grilling, baking and dry-frying.
- Baste meat and fish with tomato juice or wine rather than fat.
- Use mayonnaise sparingly in dishes such as coleslaw.

How much Fat?

The general recommendation of a number of authoritative bodies is that fat should provide about 30 per cent of our dietary energy. Studies show that many people have over 40 per cent of their daily kilojoules supplied by fat. A 30-per-cent-fat diet means you eat:

- Small portions of lean meats and trim them well.
- No skin of chicken.
- Low-fat salad dressings.
- Low-fat cheeses.

Have these with plenty of fruit, vegetables, legumes and cereal grains. Is this hard to achieve?

3
The Recipes

Introduction

These recipes express the joy of combining the novel with the familiar to make cooking and eating a pleasurable and above all ... a **healthy** experience. They have all been especially created so that you, the cook, can put into practice the nutritional principles outlined in this book.

They are simple to prepare and have all been thoroughly tested. Not only are the ingredients in each recipe kept to a minimum, they are also listed in the order in which they appear in the method. All the ingredients are readily available from most supermarkets. Although most of the recipes are designed for **four**, quantities can easily be increased or reduced as required. For many of the recipes any surplus can be refrigerated or frozen to use later.

The unique feature of the recipes is the way they have been arranged into two coloured sections — **Row 1** in green and **Row 2** in yellow comprising foods listed in the top two rows of the **Healthy Diet Triangle**. The only ingredients in the recipes from Row 3 and Row 4 of the Triangle are a token number of eggs, a little sugar, cheese, wine or brandy for extra flavour and texture. These won't do us any harm in moderation.

53

The recipes have been created to provide you with some tasty and nutritious alternatives to your usual meals and snacks. They are all low in fat, salt and/or high in dietary fibre. Although most of the ingredients are made up of fresh food, there are also some processed foods, such as unsalted canned vegetables, frozen vegetables and dehydrated tomato flakes. These convenience foods deserve a place in the healthy diet of the 1980s.

Inspired by a wide variety of sources, some of the recipes are borrowed from friends, or are old family favourites. Others are international in flavour and are based on Lebanese, Italian, Greek and Asian dishes. Whatever their origin the recipes have all been adapted to take account of the nutrition principles in this book.

Is healthy living your goal? These recipes will set you on the path.

Good health!

List of Recipes

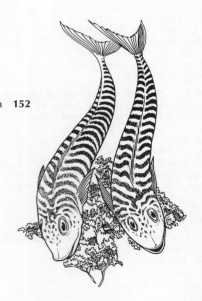

Row 1 — Breakfasts

Fruit Whip Drink

Sometimes you don't feel like eating breakfast, you're in a hurry or need something light before you go for your early-morning swim or jog. This delicious fruity drink is a novel way to start the day and takes only a minute or so to prepare. You can adjust the proportions of fruit to suit your own taste.

Ingredients

fruit juice — apple, orange, grape

fruit in season — peaches, nectarines, pears, raspberries, strawberries, plums, oranges, mangoes

natural low-fat yoghurt

Method

- Place required amount of fruit juice in blender.
- Add one or more varieties of fresh fruit and low-fat yoghurt to taste.
- Blend until puréed.
- Serve chilled in tall glass with a slice of lemon or a sprig of mint.

Fruity Muesli

Switzerland is the birth-place of this world-famous dish. It has undergone many changes from the original rolled oats and fruit, and the commercial varieties are often very high in sugar. It is much more fun to make your own home-made version from the wide range of nuts and fruit available. Serve with freshly grated apple and low-fat yoghurt or milk.

Ingredients

560 g (1¼ lb) rolled oats

115 g (4 oz) bran, processed or unprocessed

60 g (2 oz) coconut (use shredded variety)

115 g (4 oz) currants

60 g (2 oz) wheatgerm

60 g (2 oz) sunflower seeds

30 g (1 oz) sesame seeds

1 pkt (110 g, 3–4 oz) flaked almonds (or crushed peanuts)

1 pkt (200 g, 6–7 oz) mixed dried fruit

Method

- Mix together in a large bowl.
- Keep in airtight jar.
- Try toasting the rolled oats for variety before adding remaining ingredients.

Rolled Oats with Currants and Bran

This is not a porridge in the traditional sense which for many of us conjures up childhood memories of a lumpy and colourless mixture. This nourishing dish is really a hot muesli. Cooking bran with rolled oats in this way makes a digestible and high-fibre start to the day. The currants give it a fruity flavour and reduce the need for added sugar. Try adding stewed apples or apricots for variety.

Ingredients

560 g, (1¼ lb) rolled oats

115 g (4 oz) currants

115 g (4 oz) bran

2 dessertspoons skim milk powder

750 ml (1¼ pts) water

Method

- Place all ingredients in a saucepan.
- Bring to boil and cook for 2 to 3 minutes until thickened.
- Serve with low-fat milk or natural low-fat yoghurt.

Toasted Muesli

Currants and sultanas add natural sweetness to this crunchy muesli. It is delicious served with sliced banana or apricot and low-fat milk.

Ingredients

450 g (1 lb) good quality rolled oats

115 g (4 oz) unprocessed bran

60 g (2 oz) processed bran

1 tablespoon wheatgerm

225 g (8 oz) currants

225 g (8 oz) sultanas

2 tablespoons pumpkin seeds (pepitas)

60 g (2 oz) sunflower seeds

1 tablespoon pine nuts

Method

- Spread oats on a scone tray and bake at 150°C (300°F) until lightly browned. Cool.
- Place in a bowl and add remaining ingredients.
- Keep in an airtight container and use as required.

Row 1 — Soups

Apricot Wine Soup

This fruit soup is a rich amber colour. It makes a light and refreshing start or finish to a meal. It is also delicious mixed with your favourite muesli for breakfast — just omit the wine and add more fruit juice. Feel free to be as creative as you like.

Ingredients

225 g (8 oz) dried apricots

500 ml (1 pt) orange or apple juice

250 ml (½ pt) white wine

250 ml (½ pt) low-fat natural yoghurt

Method

- Soak the apricots in fruit juice and wine until softened — at least 1 hour.
- Place in blender with yoghurt and blend well.
- Chill.
- Garnish soup with a teaspoon of yoghurt and a mint sprig.

Cauliflower Soup

A delicious creamy soup without cream. This recipe is quick and easy to prepare. It may be varied by using either celery or broccoli. Milk could be used instead of chicken stock and one beaten egg can be added just before serving for extra nourishment.

Ingredients

1 small cauliflower, washed and cut into florets

1 tablespoon low-salt polyunsaturated margarine

2 tablespoons flour

1.5 litre (3 pt) chicken stock

black pepper

nutmeg

parsley, chopped

Method

- Melt margarine in a large saucepan.
- Stir in the flour.
- Add chicken stock slowly to prevent lumps forming and stir until mixture thickens.
- Add cauliflower.
- Bring to boil and cook for 10 minutes.
- Place in blender and purée until smooth.
- Add pepper and nutmeg to taste.
- Stir in parsley just before serving.

Fruit Salad Soup

What could be more appealing after the savoury course on a hot day that this flavoursome fruit soup. You can vary the fruit you use depending on what is in season.

Ingredients

2 pears

2 apricots

1 banana

1 punnet strawberries

250 ml (½ pt) water

juice of half lemon

1 400 g (13 oz approximately) can unsweetened peaches

125 ml (¼ pt) white wine

Method

- Wash fruit. Peel, core and stone as required, chopping fruit into pieces.
- Place fruit in a saucepan with water and lemon juice.
- Add canned peaches and juice.
- Cover and simmer for 10–15 minutes until tender.
- Allow to cool and place in a blender and purée.
- Add wine and more water if necessary.
- Chill thoroughly before serving.
- Garnish with finely sliced strawberries and chopped mint.

Old-Fashioned Pea Soup

A meal on its own when served with hot crusty rye bread. A cup of thinly sliced Vienna sausage added at the last moment for flavour and texture makes it a delicious treat.

Ingredients

1 carrot, washed and sliced

2 onions, chopped

1 stick of celery, chopped

1 dessertspoon polyunsaturated oil

2 bacon bones

225 g (8 oz) split peas

1.5 litres (3 pt) chicken stock

2 tablespoons parsley, chopped

Method

- Heat oil in a saucepan and gently fry vegetables until onion is transparent.
- Add bacon bones, peas and chicken stock.
- Bring to boil and simmer for 1 hour until split peas are soft (20 minutes in pressure cooker).
- Serve sprinkled with parsley.

Parsnip and Broccoli Soup

This soup is reminiscent of a vegetable mulligatawney, the curry powder gives it a delicate spicy flavour. It makes an unusual starter to a meal or a nutritious Sunday-evening snack when served with crusty wholemeal bread or rolls.

Ingredients

1 tablespoon polyunsaturated oil

2 onions, chopped

1 teaspoon curry powder

4 large parsnips, washed and sliced

450 g (1 lb) broccoli, chopped

1 litre (2 pt) chicken stock (or 750 ml stock, 250 ml milk)

black pepper

nutmeg

chives, chopped

Method

- Place oil in a saucepan and cook onion until lightly browned.
- Add curry powder, parsnips, broccoli, chicken stock and black pepper.
- Bring to boil and simmer until vegetables are just tender.
- Place in food processor or blender and process until smooth.
- Return to saucepan and warm through, adding nutmeg to taste.
- Sprinkle with chives and serve hot.

Pearl Barley Soup

This is a meal in a bowl. A soup to bring back childhood memories — just like mother used to make. Served with toasted cheese and fresh vegetable fingers, it makes a satisfying 'Sunday-night-by-the-fire' meal. It keeps well for a few days in the refrigerator.

Ingredients

150 g (5 oz) barley, soaked and drained

2 litres (4 pt) chicken or beef stock

1 bay leaf

2 large onions, sliced

2 turnips, diced

4 large carrots, diced

4 medium potatoes, diced

ground black pepper

2 tablespoons parsley, chopped

Method

- Simmer the pearl barley, with the bay leaf in the stock in a large covered saucepan for ¾ hour.

- Add the vegetables, season with pepper and simmer 10−15 minutes or until just cooked.

- Remove the bay leaf and serve garnished with parsley.

Spiced Cherry Soup

A spicy colourful soup — delicious for summer breakfasts with friends, as a starter to a meal or as a dessert. Served with a spoonful of yoghurt and garnished with lemon slices it is an irresistible treat.

Ingredients

450 g (1 lb) dark cherries

3 tablespoons tapioca

rind of half a lemon

6 whole cloves

stick cinnamon

2 dessertspoons sugar

5 cups water

315 ml (⅝ pt) red wine

thin lemon slices

Method

- Wash cherries, remove stones and stems.
- Cover tapioca with water and set aside.
- Cut lemon rind into 6 strips.
- Stick cloves into lemon rind.
- In large saucepan combine cherries, lemon rind, cinnamon stick, sugar and water.
- Drain tapioca, gradually add to cherry mixture and bring to boil. Simmer until the mixture is clear.
- Remove from heat. Stir in wine and allow to cool.
- Discard lemon rind, cloves and cinnamon.
- Refrigerate for several hours.
- Garnish with lemon slices.

Summer Soup (Gazpacho)

This easy-to-prepare version of a traditional Spanish soup is served chilled. It is the ideal start to a meal on a hot day and looks decorative served in a large soup tureen with cubes of ice floating on the surface.

Ingredients

1 can (400 g or 13 oz approximately) peeled unsalted tomatoes

¼ green capsicum

½ continental cucumber, unpeeled

2 stalks celery, sliced

3 sprigs parsley

⅓ clove garlic

250 ml (½ pt) cold water

1 tablespoon tarragon vinegar

2 tablespoons olive oil

black pepper

Method

- Place all ingredients in a blender and blend for 15 seconds.
- Chill and serve decorated with extra chopped parsley.

Sweet Corn Chowder

This is a thick soup with a slightly chewy texture and can be made in a minute or two. It looks pretty garnished with plenty of freshly chopped parsley which also complements the flavour of the sweet corn.

Ingredients

1 tablespoon low-fat polyunsaturated margarine

2 onions, finely chopped

1 tablespoon plain flour

750 ml (1½ pt) low-fat milk

1 cup sweet corn kernels (frozen, fresh or canned)

1 cup parsley, chopped

Method

- Melt margarine in saucepan.
- Add onions and cook until transparent.
- Stir in flour until well blended.
- Remove saucepan from heat and slowly stir in milk.
- Add sweet corn and bring mixture to boil then simmer for 5 minutes.
- Stir parsley through and serve hot.

Row 1 — Vegetables (Hot and Cold)

Apple Cabbage Slaw

The brightly coloured apple skins and dark sultanas give this coleslaw an attractive appearance. Add pieces of chilled cooked chicken or salmon to make a light, nutritious meal.

Ingredients

450 g (1 lb) shredded cabbage (use a mixture of red and white)

3 red apples, quartered and chopped

225 g (8 oz) sultanas

2 tablespoons parsley, chopped

Method

- Place all ingredients in a bowl and stir salad dressing through.
- Chill and serve.

Dressing Ingredients

1 tablespoon polyunsaturated oil

1 tablespoon vinegar or lemon juice

½ teaspoon prepared mustard

Method

- Place in a screw-top jar and shake to mix.

Baked Onions with Cheese Topping

Onions cooked in this way retain their sweet flavour and crunchy texture. Delicious served with roast meat, jacket potatoes and a fresh green salad.

Ingredients

4 onions

1 slice wholemeal bread

2 tablespoons grated low-fat cheese

1 dessertspoon fresh herbs, chopped — basil, thyme or oregano

Method

- Peel onions and cut in half.
- Crumble bread and mix with cheese and herbs.
- Sprinkle over onions which have been placed in a small ovenproof dish.
- Bake at 180°C (350°F) for 30 minutes.

Cheesy Vegetables

This dish is like a vegetable fruit salad — the variety in taste, texture and colour give it a special magic. For extra eye appeal, serve it in a glass bowl to display the vegetables to full effect. You may substitute any other vegetable in season, such as courgettes.

Ingredients

potatoes

carrots

peas

cabbage

pumpkin

tasty cheese for sprinkling

parsley

Method

- Cut washed, unpeeled carrots and potatoes into 2 cm (1 in) cubes or chunks. Peel and cube pumpkin.

- Cut cabbage into approx 2 cm (1 in) squares.

- Place vegetables in a steamer in the following order: potatoes, carrots, pumpkin, cabbage, then peas.

- Steam over boiling water until cooked but still crunchy.

- Pile in a serving dish. Sprinkle with cheese and parsley and serve hot.

Cherry and Cucumber Salad

An unusual and refreshing summer salad which goes well with cold meats and grills, or with cottage cheese for a light lunch.

Ingredients

½ unpeeled cucumber, cubed

225 g (8 oz) cherries, washed and stoned

1 stalk celery, washed and diced

French dressing

lettuce leaves

Method

- Combine cucumber, cherries and celery.
- Pour French dressing over and toss well.
- Serve on a bed of shredded lettuce leaves.

Cucumber Salad

This crunchy textured and colourful salad is always eaten to the last sultana. It is a must at a buffet luncheon and 'bring-a-plate' parties.

Ingredients

225 g (8 oz) unpeeled cucumber, diced

225 g (8 oz) unpeeled red apple, diced

1 cup celery, diced

4 tablespoons sultanas

4 tablespoons almonds, whole, unpeeled or slivered

4 tablespoons parsley, chopped

Method

- Combine all ingredients except a few almonds to reserve for garnish.
- Add dressing and serve chilled.

Dressing Ingredients

1 dessertspoon polyunsaturated mayonnaise

2 dessertspoons vinegar

2 dessertspoons polyunsaturated vegetable oil

¼ teaspoon mustard

Method

- Shake all ingredients together in a jar.

Curry Sauce

This curry sauce is delicious mixed with an assortment of lightly steamed vegetables and served on a bed of brown rice. It can also be served with steamed fish or chicken. It is quick and easy to prepare and makes a highly nutritious one-pot meal.

Ingredients

60 g (2 oz) sultanas

60 g (2 oz) low-salt polyunsaturated margarine

1 onion, chopped

1 tablespoon curry powder

2 tablespoons plain flour

2 carrots, thinly sliced

2 cooking apples, peeled and sliced

250 ml (½ pt) low-fat milk

250 ml (½ pt) vegetable stock

2 bay leaves

Method

- Soak sultanas for 1 hour in water and drain.
- Melt margarine and fry onion until transparent.
- Stir in curry powder and flour. Cook for 2 minutes, stirring continuously.
- Add remaining ingredients. Bring to boil, cover and simmer for ½ hour.

Glazed Carrots

Here is a quick and easy way to retain the flavour and colour of cooked carrots. Use orange juice instead of stock and sugar for a change. The almonds give the carrots a delicious crunchy topping.

Ingredients

4 carrots

1 teaspoon sugar

1 teaspoon polyunsaturated margarine

chicken stock to cover

2 tablespoons mint, chopped

toasted almonds

Method

- Scrub carrots and slice very finely.
- Place in saucepan and just cover with chicken stock.
- Add margarine and sugar. Cover and bring to boil.
- Remove lid and boil on high until all liquid has evaporated and carrots are glazed.
- Stir mint through carrots.
- Place in serving dish and top with almonds.

Parsley Salad (Tabbouleh)

This traditional Lebanese salad is becoming increasingly popular. Pita bread pockets stuffed with tabbouleh make an excellent portable lunch for hikes in the country. Burghul is pre-cooked, cracked wheat and needs only soaking to be ready for use. Serve with meat loaf, Lebanese bread and hoummus, barbecued meat, chicken, fish or cottage cheese.

Ingredients

225 g (8 oz) burghul

1 bunch parsley

2 spring onions, chopped

2 sprigs mint, chopped

generous sprinkle of allspice, cinnamon, nutmeg

60 ml (⅛ pt) lemon juice

1 clove garlic, crushed

60 ml (⅛ pt) polyunsaturated vegetable oil

black pepper

2 small tomatoes, finely chopped

Method

- Soak burghul in hot water for 1 hour — drain.
- Mix burghul, parsley, onion, mint and spices together.
- Shake lemon juice, garlic, pepper and vegetable oil together. Mix through salad.
- Chop tomatoes finely and gently stir through salad.

Potato Salad

The ubiquitous potato salad! This hearty dish is adapted from a German recipe. The yoghurt has been substituted for cream to make a lighter and more nutritious salad.

Ingredients

4 potatoes, unpeeled

2 green apples, unpeeled

1 hard-boiled egg

1 tablespoon polyunsaturated mayonnaise

1 tablespoon low-fat yoghurt

2 tablespoons parsley, chopped

Method

- Steam potatoes. Cool and cut into small pieces.
- Boil eggs for 10 minutes. Peel egg and cut into small pieces.
- Cut apples into small cubes.
- Mix all ingredients together and serve on shredded lettuce leaves.

Spinach with Pine Nuts

This tasty dish is Italian in origin. It is really delicious — nothing like the watery green mush we refused to eat as children. Here is a dish to tempt the most hardened spinach-hater. It is full of iron too.

Ingredients

450 g (1 lb) spinach, cooked, well-drained and chopped

2 tablespoons pine nuts

1 dessertspoon polyunsaturated low-salt margarine

1 dessertspoon plain flour

1/8 teaspoon nutmeg

pinch of dehydrated garlic flakes

freshly ground black pepper to taste

grated Parmesan cheese

Method

- Place cooked spinach in a casserole dish.
- Stir through pine nuts.
- Melt margarine in a saucepan.
- Add flour and cook for 1 minute over medium heat.
- Remove from heat and add milk very slowly
- Return saucepan to stove and cook until sauce thickens, stirring until a thick custard consistency.
- Add nutmeg, garlic and pepper.
- Pour over spinach mixture.
- Sprinkle with grated Parmesan cheese.
- Bake in a moderate oven 190°C (375°F) until heated through — approximately 10 minutes.

Stuffed Baked Potatoes

The humble potato is a highly versatile vegetable, and cooked in this way has added fibre. It can be served as a main course with salad or used as a vegetable with meat. For variety you can also add sunflower seeds, sesame seeds, chopped cooked bacon, nuts, celery, tomato or whatever combination you like.

Ingredients

2 large potatoes

1 onion, chopped

2 mushrooms, chopped

2 tablespoons parsley, chopped

60 g (2 oz) low-fat cheese, grated

black pepper

Method

- Scrub potatoes and bake in a moderate oven 190°C (375°F) for 1 hour until soft.
- Fry chopped onion in a little oil until transparent. Add mushrooms and cook for 2 minutes.
- Scoop out centres of potatoes leaving small amount around skin for support.
- Mash potato, add onion, mushrooms, parsley, most of the grated cheese and pepper. Place in potato shells and sprinkle remaining cheese on top.
- Bake in a moderate oven 20 minutes until nicely browned on top.

Tomato Jelly

This sharp-flavoured jelly makes an ideal entrée or an accompaniment to a cold buffet. Although we often associate jellies with the dessert course, they also lend themselves to a variety of savoury courses as this recipe demonstrates. Served on a white plate and garnished with sprigs of parsley or watercress, this dish can be used for just about any occasion.

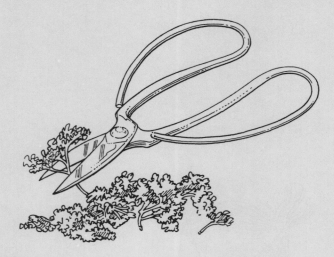

Ingredients

1 800 g (1¾ lb) can peeled unsalted tomatoes

1 teaspoon sugar

1 tablespoon tomato flakes

½ teaspoon dried garlic flakes

3 bay leaves

2−3 drops Tabasco sauce

black pepper

125 ml (¼ pt) water

125 ml (¼ pt) dry white wine

30 g (1 oz) powdered gelatine

Method

- Place canned tomatoes in a food processor or blender and purée until smooth.

- Pour into a saucepan with sugar, tomato flakes, garlic, bay leaves, Tabasco and black pepper and bring to the boil. Remove from heat and discard bay leaves.

- Place water and wine in a small saucepan and sprinkle gelatine over liquid. Leave to soak for 1 minute.

- Place saucepan on stove and heat gently until liquid becomes clear.

- Mix with tomato mixture to make 1 litre (4 cups) of liquid and stir thoroughly.

- Pour into a lightly oiled mould and chill until set.

- Turn out on a plate and garnish with parsley or watercress.

Wheat and Onion Salad

This colourful salad takes very little time to prepare and will keep in the refrigerator for 2 to 3 days. It goes particularly well with cold meats for an easy summer meal.

Salad Ingredients

345 g (12 oz) quick-cooking rolled wheat

315 ml (5/8 pt) hot water

1 level teaspoon polyunsaturated margarine

225 g (8 oz) walnuts or pecan nuts, chopped

2 spring onions, sliced

2 tomatoes, diced

1 stalk celery, sliced

2 tablespoons parsley, finely chopped

Method

- Place rolled wheat, water and margarine in saucepan. Bring to boil.
- Reduce heat and simmer for 10–12 minutes, by which time wheat will be cooked and water evaporated. Cool.
- Mix all ingredients together. Stir through dressing.
- Chill and serve.

Dressing Ingredients

2 dessertspoons white wine vinegar

2 dessertspoons polyunsaturated vegetable oil

1 clove garlic (optional)

black pepper

Method

- Mix together in a small container and shake until well blended.

Courgette Salad

Raw courgettes make an excellent salad vegetable, especially if they are small and fresh, as they are sweet and tender. Courgette tends to be easier to digest than cucumber and can be substituted for it in salads.

Ingredients

4 small courgettes, finely sliced

6 button mushrooms, finely sliced

4 tablespoons parsley, chopped

1 cup Tom Thumb tomatoes

Method

- Mix vegetables together in a salad bowl.
- Shake dressing ingredients together and pour over vegetables. Stir gently.
- Chill and serve.

Dressing Ingredients

1 dessertspoon polyunsaturated vegetable oil

1 dessertspoon vinegar

small clove garlic (optional)

pinch paprika

Method

- Mix together in a bowl and pour over salad.

Row 1 — Main Meals (Lunches and Dinners)

Cheese and Basil Sauce for Pasta

This cheese and basil sauce is reminiscent of the famous Italian pesto sauce. Always use fresh herbs — dried are no substitute and there's nothing quite like a sprinkling of freshly grated cheese on top of the dish for extra flavour.

Ingredients

2 onions, sliced

1 tablespoon polyunsaturated margarine

1 tablespoon plain flour

500 ml (1 pt) low-fat milk

115 g (4 oz) tasty cheese, grated

black pepper

fresh basil, chopped

2 tablespoons pine nuts

Method

- Melt margarine in saucepan, add onions and cook gently until transparent.
- Stir in flour, cook for 1 minute.
- Remove from heat and add milk, cheese and pepper.
- Return to stove, cook until bubbling, stirring constantly.
- Pour over cooked pasta and stir lightly.
- Sprinkle with basil and pine nuts and stir through.

Aubergine Stew with Chick Peas

This popular Middle-Eastern favourite can be used as a main meal or a vegetable. It can be served hot or cold, and is delicious with a generous sprinkling of parsley and warmed, Lebanese bread.

Ingredients

1 large aubergine, washed and sliced

1 tablespoon olive oil

1 onion, finely chopped

1 clove garlic, crushed

400 g (13 oz approximately) can peeled unsalted tomatoes, chopped

225 g (8 oz) cooked chick peas

black pepper

oregano to taste

parsley

Method

- Sprinkle aubergine with salt to remove bitter juices. Leave for 20 minutes, then wash and dry carefully.

- Place olive oil in a saucepan, add onion and garlic and cook until transparent.

- Add tomatoes, chick peas, pepper, oregano and aubergine and simmer until aubergine is cooked and all flavours are well blended — approximately 15 minutes.

- Place in a bowl and sprinkle liberally with chopped parsley.

Fried Rice

This delicious oriental recipe can be varied enormously depending on what takes your fancy. Tasty, chewy wholegrain rice is far more nutritious than white rice and the dish needs only a bowl of stir-fried vegetables to become a main meal.

Ingredients

225 g (8 oz) brown rice

2 large onions

1 tablespoon polyunsaturated oil

2 rashers bacon, diced

225 g (8 oz) frozen peas

115 g (4 oz) bean sprouts

2 tablespoons soy sauce

2 eggs

Method

- Cook rice in boiling water for ¾ hour until soft. Drain.
- Cut up onions.
- Add oil to wok (or frypan) and cook onions until transparent.
- Add bacon, cook until crisp.
- Add frozen peas and bean sprouts and cook for 2 minutes.
- Add rice, soy sauce and two beaten eggs. Stir through until eggs are cooked.
- Serve hot and use chopsticks for fun!

Jambalaya

This is an easy to prepare version of the Creole recipe from America's Deep South and is a marvellous one-dish meal. A handful of prawns may be added with the chicken for a touch of extravagance. It looks marvellous served with a green salad and garnished with black olives. Refrigerate any leftovers and reheat the next day, adding a tablespoon or two of water.

Ingredients

225 g (8 oz) brown rice

1 large onion, chopped

1 dessertspoon polyunsaturated oil

1 chicken breast, finely diced

1 400 g (13 oz approximately) can peeled unsalted tomatoes, blended

pinch cayenne pepper

1 ham steak, finely diced

pinch chilli powder (optional)

Method

- Cook rice in boiling water until tender. Drain.
- Fry onion in oil until transparent.
- Add chicken and cook, stirring, for approximately 5 minutes until cooked.
- Add remaining ingredients and heat through.
- Garnish with parsley before serving.

Mexican Spoon Bread

Freshly baked, this bread fills the kitchen with the most wonderful aroma. It is adapted from a Mexican dish, using low-fat cheese and substituting onions for chillis. Easy and quick to prepare, it can form the basis of a spur-of-the-moment meal with friends. By all means use chillis — if you dare!

Ingredients

300 g (approximately 10½ oz) can creamed corn

125 ml (¼ pt) low-fat milk

4 tablespoons polyunsaturated vegetable oil

2 eggs, lightly beaten

115 g (4 oz) polenta (corn meal)

2 teaspoons baking powder

2 large onions, chopped

175 g (6 oz) low-fat cheese, grated

Method

- Blend corn, milk, oil and eggs in a bowl.
- Add polenta and baking powder.
- Stir in chopped onion and most of the cheese, retaining a little to sprinkle on top of dish.
- Pour batter into an oiled baking dish.
- Sprinkle with remaining cheese.
- Bake 45−55 minutes at 350°F (180°C). Serve hot with a green salad.

Pasta with Broccoli and Pine Nuts

Pasta is an excellent base for creative sauces. Although many Italian sauces are made with cream, this one, like most in this book, is based on white sauce made with low-fat milk. Green peppercorns can be added for extra zest. Try experimenting with your favourite herbs and spices.

Ingredients

175 g (6 oz) broccoli, washed and trimmed

1 tablespoon low-salt polyunsaturated margarine

2 onions, chopped

1 tablespoon flour

500 ml (1 pt) low-fat milk

90 g (3 oz) tasty cheese, grated

black pepper

225 g (8 oz) shell pasta

2 tablespoons pine nuts

Parmesan cheese, for sprinkling

parsley, chopped

Method

- Steam broccoli until barely cooked. Drain and chop.
- Cook noodles according to instructions on packet.
- Melt margarine in saucepan, add onions and cook until transparent.
- Add flour and cook until bubbling.
- Remove from heat, add milk and pepper. Cook over medium heat until thickened.
- Add broccoli, cheese and pine nuts and stir through noodles.
- Serve hot, sprinkled with Parmesan cheese and parsley.

96

Pecan Noodle Bake

This dish takes a little more time to prepare than most of the other recipes in the book. However, the effort is worth it. Served with crusty bread, a colourful tossed salad and a bottle of wine, it makes a tempting special-occasion dish. You can make it in two small casserole dishes and freeze one for later use.

Ingredients

345 g (12 oz) noodles (shell pasta, macaroni, et cetera)

2 onions, chopped

1 dessertspoon polyunsaturated oil

1 800 g (approximately 1¾ lb) can peeled, unsalted tomatoes, chopped

2 courgettes, sliced

black pepper

1 teaspoon dried basil or oregano

115 g (4 oz) pecan nuts

Method

- Cook noodles for required amount of time in boiling water.
- Drain and spread over bottom of two small casserole dishes.
- Cook chopped onions in oil.
- Add tomatoes, courgettes, pepper and basil.
- Cook uncovered until courgettes are just tender.
- Add pecan nuts.
- Pour mixture over noodles in casserole dishes.
- Cover with cheese sauce (see over) and bake at 375°F (190°C) for approx. 30 minutes or until top turns golden brown.

Cheese Sauce Ingredients

1 tablespoon low-salt polyunsaturated margarine

1 tablespoon plain flour

375 ml (¾ pt) low-fat milk

60 g (2 oz) low-fat cheese

Method

- Melt margarine and add flour.
- Cook for one minute.
- Add milk and cheese and bring to boil.
- Cook gently for 3 minutes.
- Pour over tomato mixture.

Potato Pancakes

This recipe is adapted from the Jewish recipe for latkes (raw potato pancakes) — the traditional treat for the festival of Hanukah. The pancakes are crunchy and delicious. A tasty accompaniment is cranberry, apple or plum sauce and a colourful salad such as lettuce with orange slices, raw sliced courgettes and tomato wedges.

Ingredients

4 large potatoes, grated

1 small onion, grated

1 small egg, beaten

2 tablespoons flour

pepper

polyunsaturated oil for frying

Method

- Place potatoes and onions in a sieve and squeeze out excess moisture. Place in a bowl.
- Stir in egg, flour and pepper and mix with a fork.
- Heat oil over medium heat in a frying pan.
- Drop tablespoon lots in hot oil, flatten with a spoon.
- Fry for approximately 4 minutes until golden brown.
- Flip over and fry for a further 4 minutes.
- Drain on paper towels.

Savoury Pumpkin Pie

This nutty flavoured pie has been adapted from the Stuffed Pumpkin recipe (next). The combination of a crunchy pie crust with a creamy pumpkin filling gives it an unusual texture. The only addition it needs is a crisp lettuce salad.

Pumpkin Mixture Ingredients

1 small pumpkin, peeled

2 large onions

1 dessertspoon polyunsaturated oil

2 dessertspoons sunflower seeds

2 tablespoons parsley, chopped

115 g (4 oz) low-fat cheese

2 eggs, beaten

1 teaspoon dried oregano or marjoram

2 dessertspoons sesame seeds

Method

- Steam pumpkin until soft. Mash while warm.
- Fry onions in oil until transparent.
- Stir in pumpkin.
- Add remaining ingredients except sesame seeds.

Pastry Ingredients

2 cups flour (all wholemeal or half white and half wholemeal)

6 tablespoons margarine

2 tablespoons water

juice of a lemon

Method

- Rub margarine into flour.
- Add water and lemon juice and mix well together.
- Add more water if necessary — knead for a while and roll out to fit two 25 cm (10 in) pie plates.
- Fill with pumpkin mixture and sprinkle top with sesame seeds.
- Bake at 190°C (375°F) for 20–30 minutes or until pastry is cooked and sesame seeds browned.

Stuffed Pumpkin

This is an easy to prepare vegetarian dish as well as an imaginative way to use pumpkin. The appetising combination of colour, texture and flavour appeals to dedicated meat-eaters as well. You can make double quantities and freeze the remainder for later use.

Ingredients

1 small pumpkin

2 onions, chopped

1 teaspoon polyunsaturated oil

115 g (4 oz) cooked brown rice

1 egg, beaten

2 tablespoons sunflower seeds

black pepper

60 g (2 oz) grated low-fat cheese

2 tablespoons parsley, chopped

Method

- Cut pumpkin in half, scoop out seeds and bake in a moderate oven for 1 hour or until soft.
- Scoop out flesh, leaving 1 cm (½ in) around the inside of the skin.
- Mash pumpkin.
- Fry onions in oil until soft.
- Mix together mashed pumpkin, onion, rice, egg, sunflower seeds, pepper, cheese and parsley.
- Fill pumpkin shells with mixture.
- Sprinkle with a little extra cheese.
- Bake for 20–30 minutes at 375°F (190°C) until brown on top.

Tomato Sauce for Pasta

This sauce has a piquant flavour and makes a superb topping for wholemeal pasta. Keep a supply of noodles, canned tomatoes, onions, herbs and grated Parmesan cheese handy — you will always have the basic ingredients for a tasty meal on hand. You can use a variety of ingredients such as carrot, olives, cabbage, aubergine, mushrooms, minced chicken or whatever takes your fancy.

Ingredients

1 large onion, chopped

1 clove garlic, crushed

1 dessertspoon polyunsaturated oil

1 400 g (approximately 13 oz) can peeled unsalted tomatoes

1 courgette, sliced or diced

1 bay leaf

black pepper

2 dessertspoons dehydrated tomato flakes

1 teaspoon dried basil or oregano

2 tablespoons parsley, chopped

Pecorino Romano or Parmesan cheese for sprinkling over dish.

Method

- Cook onion and garlic in oil until transparent.
- Mash or blend tomatoes and add to onion.
- Add courgette, bay leaf, basil or oregano, pepper and tomato flakes and bring to the boil.
- Simmer 15 minutes.
- Pour over cooked pasta and mix lightly together.
- Stir in parsley.

Row 1 — Fruit Desserts and Wholegrain Baked Products

Apple Buns

These apple buns are a much healthier version of Chelsea buns. They are low in sugar and fat and can be varied by using chopped nuts and orange peel instead of sultanas.

Scone Dough Ingredients

345 g (12 oz) self-raising flour (half wholemeal, half white)

45 g (1½ oz) low-salt margarine

250 ml (½ pt) low-fat milk

polyunsaturated oil

Method

- Sift flour into a bowl. Add margarine and rub in lightly.
- Add milk and mix to a firm dough.
- Roll into a rectangle approximately 30 cm × 23 cm (12 in × 9 in).
- Brush with a little oil.
- Sprinkle with apple and sultana mixture. (See below.)
- Roll up lengthwise, sealing join with a little water.
- Cut into twelve slices and place in a 23 cm (9 in) greased pie plate.
- Bake for 25–30 minutes at 190°C (375°F).

Filling Ingredients

2 large Granny Smith apples

225 g (8 oz) sultanas

2 teaspoons mixed spice

Method

- Peel and core apples and chop into 1 cm (½ in) cubes.
- Mix in a bowl with sultanas and spice.

Basic Bread

Bread can justifiably be called 'the staff of life' — we should all be eating more of it. This bread has the light texture of white bread combined with the fibre of brown. It is very easy to make and can be varied with the addition of soya flour, wheatgerm and sunflower seeds for extra protein and a more grainy texture.

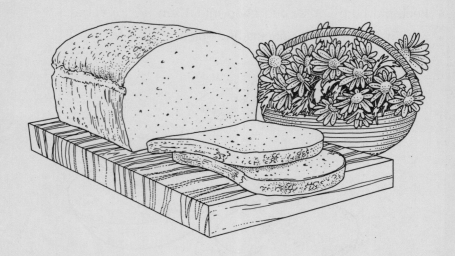

Ingredients

450 g (1 lb) wholemeal bread flour

450 g (1 lb) white bread flour (available at groceries and health food shops)

1 teaspoon salt

4 teaspoons dried yeast (available at groceries and health food shops)

2 teaspoons yeast improver (available at groceries and health food shops)

2 tablespoons polyunsaturated oil

875 ml–1 litre (1¾–2 pt) hand-hot water

Method

- Sift flour, salt, yeast and improver together into a large bowl.

- Stir oil into water and pour into a well in the centre of the flour.

- Mix until you have a soft (not dry) mixture. Knead on a floured board for 5 minutes or until very springy.

- Shape and place in 2 tins, or 'braid' and place on trays.

- Place in a warm place to rise until double in size — 20–30 minutes.

- Bake at 190°C (375°F) for 30 minutes or until bread sounds hollow when tapped.

Brandied Fruit

This recipe is delicious served hot with icecream or cold with low-fat yoghurt. You can experiment with other fruit combinations — adding diced apples, peaches or nectarines. Packed in decorative jars brandied fruit makes an imaginative gift for a festive occasion.

Ingredients

1 375 g (approximately 12 oz) packet pitted prunes

1 800 g (approximately 1¾ lb) can unsweetened pineapple pieces

1 400 g (approximately 13 oz) can unsweetened peach slices

1 125 g (approximately 4 oz) packet red glacé cherries

1 100 g (approximately 3 oz) packet almonds

185 ml (⅝ pt) brandy

125 ml (¼ pt) water

Method

- Drain peaches and pineapple and place in a bowl. Add cherries, almonds and brandy.
- Place juices and water in a saucepan with the prunes.
- Bring to boil and simmer for 7 minutes.
- Add to fruit in bowl.

Crunchy Orange Cup

This simple dish has a delicious ambrosial flavour and makes a refreshing change to fruit salad. It goes well with a light, chilled custard or low-fat yoghurt. Sweet juicy oranges are essential to the success of this dessert.

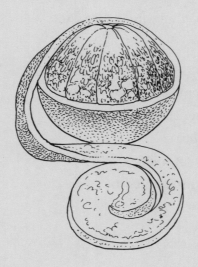

Ingredients

4 large navel oranges

60 g (2 oz) coconut (use the long shredded variety)

rum or liqueur to taste

Method

- Cut oranges into thin slices and trim off skin and pith.
- Lightly toast coconut.
- Arrange orange slices and toasted coconut in alternate layers in individual glass bowls.
- Sprinkle with rum or your favourite liqueur.
- Chill for 1 hour before serving.

Currant Muffins

This muffin recipe is one of several in this book. These wholemeal currant muffins are quick and easy to make and are a delicious addition to the breakfast or tea table. You can experiment with your own variations with different dried fruits and nuts.

Muffins freeze well and thaw quickly.

Ingredients

225 g (8 oz) wholemeal self-raising flour

2 dessertspoons raw sugar

225 g (8 oz) currants

250 ml (½ pt) low-fat milk

60 ml (⅛ pt) polyunsaturated oil

1 egg

Method

- Sift flour and sugar. Add currants.
- Beat milk, oil and egg together and mix lightly into flour mixture.
- Bake in oiled muffin pans at 190°C (375°F) for 20 minutes in the middle of the oven.
- Leave for 5 minutes before removing from pans.
- Serve hot or cold.

Festive Fruit Basket

You won't miss rich and heavy desserts when this basket of tempting fruits in season is placed before you. Whatever fresh fruit you use, always include some dried fruit for colour contrast.

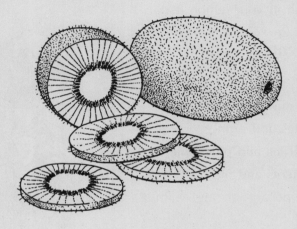

Ingredients

cherries

quarters of fresh pineapple (skin on)

honeydew melon or cantaloupe slices

watermelon slices

unhulled strawberries

kiwi fruit slices

dried figs

pitted prunes

marzipan bar, thinly sliced

Method

- Arrange attractively in a leaf lined basket.

Fruit Cake

This isn't really a recipe — it's an idea. A fruit cake without the cake. Serve it when you have friends or family for afternoon tea. It will be every bit as popular as the real thing and more colourful. If you feel deprived of the brandy in your fruit cake, put a dash in your lemon tea!

Ingredients

sultanas

muscatel raisins

pitted dates and prunes

glacé cherries and pineapple

dried apricots and figs

almonds, pecan nuts and walnuts

Method

- Arrange attractively on a large platter.

Fruit Crumble

This is an up-to-date version of an old fashioned favourite and is one of the easiest cooked desserts to make. Toasted sesame seeds can replace the coconut for those of you who are cholesterol watchers. It is delicious served hot or cold with custard or low-fat yoghurt.

Ingredients

stewed apricots, apples, plums or nectarines

Topping Ingredients

2 tablespoons wholemeal flour

2 tablespoons coconut

2 tablespoons low-salt polyunsaturated margarine

1 teaspoon cinnamon

chopped nuts if desired

Method

- Rub flour and margarine together until mixture resembles fine breadcrumbs.
- Add coconut and cinnamon and mix well.
- Place fruit in a pie dish and sprinkle with crumble mixture.
- Bake in a moderate oven 190°C (375°F) for 20 minutes or until topping is lightly browned.

Greek Rice

This version of a traditional Greek dessert uses brown rice instead of white to make a nutritious and creamy dessert. It can be served warm or cold and is especially good with sharp-flavoured stewed apricots. Why not try it for breakfast as a change from packaged cereals?

Ingredients

1 litre (2 pt) low-fat milk

115 g (4 oz) cooked brown rice

1 egg

1 dessertspoon cornflour

2 dessertspoons sugar

1 teaspoon vanilla

nutmeg or cinnamon

Method

- Bring milk to the boil, add rice and simmer for 10 minutes.
- Beat egg and mix with cornflour, sugar, vanilla and a little extra milk to mix.
- Add to milk and rice, stirring constantly until thickened.
- Pour into a bowl, sprinkle with nutmeg or cinnamon or both.

Honey Oatmeal Biscuits

This is a more nutritious version of Anzac biscuits with less sugar and more fibre. The biscuits keep well in an airtight container but can also be frozen for longer storage.

Ingredients

2 cups rolled oats

1 cup wholemeal self-raising flour

1 egg

1 teaspoon honey

1 teaspoon vanilla

2 dessertspoons sugar

115 g (4 oz) low-salt polyunsaturated margarine

Method

- Melt margarine, then add beaten egg, sugar, honey and vanilla.
- Beat for a few minutes until well blended.
- Add rolled oats and sifted self-raising flour. Mix well.
- Place in teaspoons on a cold greased slide and bake 15–20 minutes or until golden.
- Remove from tray while hot.

Marjoram Scone Savoury

This wholesome herb scone mixture has an appetising flavour. Try it with any of the soups in this book or as a light lunch-time snack with a salad and fruit.

Ingredients

450 g (1 lb) self-raising flour (half white, half wholemeal)

60 g (2 oz) polyunsaturated low-salt margarine

250 ml (½ pt) low-fat milk

Polyunsaturated vegetable oil

115 g (4 oz) low-fat cheese, grated

1 small onion, chopped

2 rashers bacon, chopped

fresh marjoram to taste

milk to glaze

poppy seeds

Method

- Sift flours and rub in margarine.
- Add milk and mix to a soft dough.
- Roll into a rectangle ½ inch (1 cm) thick.
- Brush with a little oil.
- Sprinkle with grated cheese, onion, bacon and marjoram.
- Roll up lengthwise, brush top with milk and sprinkle with poppy seeds.
- Slash top every 4 cm (1½ in) half-way through.
- Bake at 400°F (200°C) for 30–35 minutes.

Minted Fruit Salad

This tingling fruit salad is simple to make and is an excellent way to start or finish any meal. For a more exotic dish add kiwi fruit and melon and serve with mango sauce made by blending fresh mango and low-fat yoghurt together.

Ingredients

1 400 g (approximately 13 oz) can unsweetened pineapple pieces

1 banana, sliced

1 red apple, chopped finely (with skin on)

1 pear chopped finely (with skin on)

1 punnet strawberries

handful pitted prunes, cut into quarters

2 tablespoons mint, finely chopped

Mineral water

Method

- Mix all ingredients together, adding mineral water just before serving.

- Decorate with extra mint sprigs.

Moscow Piroshkis

These delicious little filled rolls have a moist savoury centre and do not need the addition of butter. They can be eaten at any time of the day — on their own or as an accompaniment to an entrée or a main course.

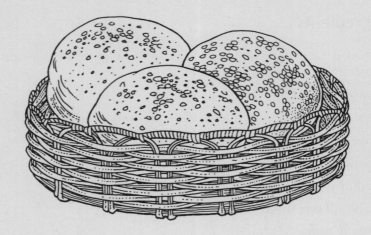

Filling Ingredients (to be made first)

2 medium-sized onions, chopped

30 g (1 oz) low-salt polyunsaturated margarine

115 g (4 oz) lean bacon, chopped

black pepper

Method

- Fry onions in margarine until golden.
- Add bacon and cook a further 5 minutes.
- Sprinkle with pepper.
- Cool.

Bread Dough Ingredients

450 g (1 lb) bread flour (half white, half wholemeal)

2 teaspoons dried yeast

1 teaspoon yeast improver

½ teaspoon salt

1 egg

1 tablespoon polyunsaturated oil

approximately 500 ml (1 pt) hand-hot water

Method

- Sift dry ingredients into a bowl.
- Mix egg, oil and water in a small bowl and pour into a well in the centre of the flour.
- Mix to a soft dough and knead for 5–10 minutes.
- Take tablespoon-sized pieces of dough, flatten or roll out and place 1 teaspoon of filling on dough.
- Fold edges in to enclose filling and form into balls.
- Place on a greased tray joined edge down, and leave to rise in a warm place for 10–15 minutes or until double in size.
- Glaze with beaten egg yolk and bake at 200°C (400°F) for 10–15 minutes.

Nutty Banana Muffins

These muffins have the flavour of banana cake but without the extra sugar. They are particularly good served straight from the oven. The aroma alone will enhance your reputation as a creative cook.

Ingredients

2 ripe bananas

1 egg

250 ml (½ pt) low-fat milk

60 ml (⅛ pt) polyunsaturated vegetable oil

225 g (8 oz) wholemeal self-raising flour

2 dessertspoons sugar

75 g (2½ oz) walnuts, chopped

Method

- Mash bananas.
- Combine egg, milk, oil and bananas in bowl, beating lightly with fork.
- Sift flour and sugar into a bowl.
- Add walnuts and make a well in the centre.
- Pour banana mixture into centre, stirring lightly until just mixed.
- Place mixture in greased muffin pans.
- Bake in a moderate oven at 375°F (190°C) for 20 minutes.
- Leave for 5 minutes before removing from pans.
- Serve hot or cold.

Oatmeal Fruit Muffins

Vive la différence! You will be enchanted by the flavour fresh fruit contributes to these high-fibre oatmeal muffins. They are simply delicious served with Fruit Spread (see page 132), or ricotta cheese.

Ingredients

175 g (6 oz) wholemeal self-raising flour

140 g (5 oz) rolled oats

2 dessertspoons raw sugar

115 g (4 oz) sultanas

1 egg

250 ml (½ pt) low-fat milk

60 ml (⅛ pt) polyunsaturated oil

225 g (8 oz) fresh fruit (blueberries, diced apple, diced peaches or combinations)

Method

- Sift flour into a bowl, adding unsifted husks as well.
- Add rolled oats, sugar and sultanas.
- Beat egg, milk and oil together then stir fresh fruit into this mixture.
- Make a well in the centre of the dry ingredients and pour in the milk mixture.
- Mix very lightly.
- Place in oiled muffin pans and bake at 190°C (375°F) for 15–20 minutes.

Seed Buns

You really can 'break bread' with friends if you serve these seed buns at a get-together. The rolls are joined in the baking process to form a large round loaf.

Ingredients

Basic Bread mixture (see page 108.)

1 egg yolk mixed with 3 tablespoons water for glazing

caraway seeds, sesame seeds, poppy seeds

Method

- Grease two 20 cm (8 in) pie plates.
- Cut dough into 34 equal sized pieces.
- Roll into small balls.
- Place two rolls in the centre of each pie plate.
- Place six rolls in a ring around the centre rolls.
- Place the last nine around the outside, squeezing them in if necessary.
- Leave to rise 15–20 minutes or until double in size.
- Brush tops lightly with egg-yolk glaze.
- Sprinkle centre with caraway seeds, middle circle with sesame seeds and outside circle with poppy seeds.
- Bake in a moderate oven 190°C (375°F) for 20 minutes or until golden brown.

Spicy Fruit Compote

Here's a novel way to serve your favourite fresh fruit. It makes a delicious light dessert or can be used as an accompaniment to meat and poultry dishes. It keeps well in the refrigerator.

Ingredients

1¼ kg (2½ lb) diced fresh fruit, washed, peeled, cored or pitted — apples, peaches, apricots, pears, nectarines

115 g (4 oz) sultanas

500 ml (1 pt) cold water (approximately)

1 dessertspoon lemon juice

⅛ teaspoon white pepper

¼ teaspoon cinnamon

⅛ teaspoon allspice

⅛ teaspoon ground cloves

Method

- Place fruit, water, lemon juice and spices in a large saucepan.
- Bring to boil and reduce heat.
- Simmer until tender but not mushy.
- Serve warm or chilled.

Tangy Apples

We sometimes forget just how versatile fruit is and the extent to which it can complement savoury dishes. This dish not only makes a light, tangy-flavoured dessert, but is also an excellent accompaniment to grilled fish, chicken or meat. Can be served hot or cold.

Ingredients

500 ml (1 pt) fresh orange juice

6 cooking apples, peeled and cored

1 teaspoon finely grated orange rind

1 tablespoon sultanas

1 tablespoon arrowroot

2 tablespoons water

Method

- Place orange juice, orange rind and sultanas in a saucepan and bring to the boil.
- Cut apples in half and add to orange juice mixture.
- Simmer gently until apples are tender but not disintegrated.
- Blend arrowroot and water to a paste.
- Add to orange mixture and cook until thickened.

Wholemeal Pumpkin Scones

These scones are rich yellow in colour and have an irresistible flavour. Try them served straight from the oven with home-made Fruit Spread (see page 132) or a little honey.

Ingredients

2 tablespoons raw sugar

45 g (1½ oz) low-salt polyunsaturated margarine

1 cup cooked pumpkin

250 ml (½ pt) low-fat milk, soured with ½ teaspoon vinegar

345 g (12 oz) wholemeal self-raising flour

Method

- Cream margarine and sugar.
- Add pumpkin and milk and mix well.
- Sift flour and stir into liquid.
- Turn dough onto a floured board, pat into shape and cut into scone shapes.
- Bake 15 minutes at 200°C (400°F).

Row 1 — Dips, Spreads and Snacks

Avocado Dip (Guacamole)

Be adventurous! If you don't like avocado or have not tasted it before, try this Mexican dip — you may be in for a pleasant surprise. Add more chilli for a hotter flavour. This dip is an excellent 'bring-a-plate' treat for a party.

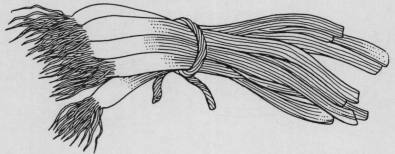

Ingredients

2 ripe avocados

2 tablespoon lemon juice

¼ teaspoon ground coriander

¼ teaspoon chilli sauce

1 small onion, finely chopped

1 tomato, finely chopped

Method

- Mash avocado with lemon juice, coriander and chilli sauce.
- Mix onion in well.
- Lightly fold in chopped tomato.
- Place in a bowl and serve with natural corn chips or raw vegetable strips.

Butter Bean Dip

This is an adaptation of the Lebanese hoummus dip, using butter beans instead of chick peas. By all means use chick peas if you prefer. This recipe makes enough for two serves — one for now and one to freeze for later.

Ingredients

1 300 g (approximately 10 oz) can butter beans

1 clove garlic

3 tablespoons tahini (sesame paste — available at delicatessens)

juice of 1 lemon

pinch cayenne pepper.

paprika

Method

- Drain butter beans, reserving liquid.
- Mince or blend butter beans.
- Add tahini, lemon juice and cayenne pepper.
- Mix briskly, adding some of the reserved liquid if necessary to make a creamy mixture.
- Place in a serving bowl and sprinkle with paprika and chopped parsley.
- Serve with Lebanese bread, tabbouleh or with biscuits as a dip.

Crêpes

Crêpes make a quick light meal and are very versatile. The variety of savoury or sweet fillings is almost endless. Try them stuffed with lightly steamed vegetables in a spicy tomato purée or alternatively with drained, home-made, fresh fruit salad.

Ingredients

2 eggs

375 ml (¾ pt) low-fat milk

3 tablespoons polyunsaturated oil

115 g (4 oz) flour (half white, half wholemeal)

Method

- Mix the eggs, milk and oil in a blender.
- Add the flour and process until smooth.
- Lightly oil a non-stick frying pan and pour in a portion of pancake batter.
- Turn when the edges have browned (about three minutes).
- Cook the other side for 2–3 minutes.
- Repeat process until all batter is used.

Danish Open Sandwiches

Here's your chance to display artistic flair. You can use just about any combination of vegetable or fruit with a savoury topping to look and taste good. Always use lightly-buttered rye bread for open sandwiches as it is firm and can be held without falling apart.

Egg and Bacon Topping

shredded lettuce

slices of egg down one side

cooked crisp bacon pieces on the other side

tomato slices topped with fresh thyme in the centre

Ham and Orange Topping

folded slices of ham

cottage or ricotta cheese

an orange twist in the centre

prunes and a sprig of parsley

Cheese and Herb Topping

slices of low-fat cheese

thin slices of cucumber

sliced raw button mushrooms

a sprinkle of fresh herbs

Fruit Spread

This spread is much more nutritious than normal sugar-laden jam. It is delicious as a topping for toast, muffins, scones, low-fat yoghurt or as a filling in wholemeal tarts. It will keep 7–10 days in the refrigerator once defrosted.

Ingredients

450 g (1 lb) fruit — apricots or peaches, apples or pears, straw-berries or raspberries, plums or gooseberries

Method

- Wash and drain fruit.
- Peel and slice if necessary.
- Place in a saucepan and cook over low heat, stirring constantly until thickened, adding a little water if necessary.
- Sweeten with a little sugar — usually 2 dessertspoons is enough.
- Place in small screw-top jars, filling to within 2 cm (1 in) of the top.
- Label and **freeze**.
- Keep in refrigerator when thawed.

Lebanese Cheese Pockets

A delicious snack to serve on its own or with soup. Pitta bread can be kept in the freezer and defrosted quickly when needed. Use your favourite salad combinations.

Ingredients

wholemeal pitta bread

tasty cheese, grated

lettuce, shredded

1 green pepper, sliced

1 cup beansprouts

vinegar

Method

- Cut pitta bread into 4 pieces. Open and fill with grated cheese.

- Warm bread in heated electric frypan until cheese melts.

- Open bread pockets and put in a handful of salad vegetables which have been sprinkled with vinegar.

Pannini

Pannini are toasted Italian snacks that taste like pizzas. You can vary the topping depending on what you have available. They are delicious served with soup for a more substantial meal.

Ingredients

wholemeal bread rolls

slices of fresh tomato

oregano

ham, chopped

mushrooms, sliced

pineapple pieces

onions, finely chopped

low-fat cheese, grated

chopped parsley

Method

- Cut bread rolls in half.
- Place a tomato slice on top, sprinkle with oregano.
- Top with ham, mushrooms, pineapple and onions.
- Cover with grated cheese.
- Grill under medium heat until cheese melts or bake at 190°C (375°F) for 10–15 minutes. Sprinkle with chopped parsley.

Sandwiches, Rolls and Crispbreads

The secret of a good sandwich is the filling, the quality of the bread and the garnish. Plain or toasted, it is acceptable fare just about anywhere from a tasty snack with friends, a portable meal at a picnic or as a dainty nibble at a special celebration.

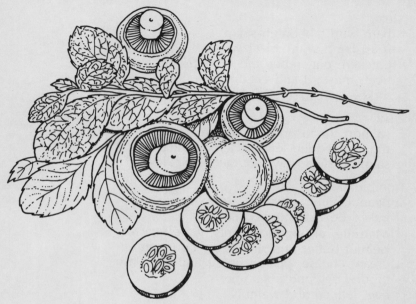

Breads

- wholemeal bread or rolls
- mixed grain bread e.g. Vogel
- rye bread
- pitta bread

Crispbread

- Ryevita
- Vitawheat

Fillings

- Cheese:
    low-fat cream cheese, dates and lettuce
    cheddar cheese with slices of apple
    cream cheese, tomato and sunflower seeds
    ricotta cheese, celery and chopped nuts

- Meat:
    ham with tabbouleh salad
    roast lamb with coleslaw
    chicken, cucumber and beansprouts
    beef, mustard and cucumber
    turkey breast, shredded lettuce and chutney

- Fish:
    salmon, beansprouts and tomato
    tuna, shredded lettuce, lemon juice
    salmon, sliced raw courgette, pickles

- Combinations:
    peanut butter, sultanas and beansprouts
    baked beans, chopped celery
    Marmite, chopped walnuts, grated carrot
    peanut butter and sliced raw courgette
    cream cheese, peanut butter and coleslaw
    curried egg and cucumber
    egg, lettuce and walnuts
    avocado, grated carrot and beansprouts

Garnishes

- sprig of mint, watercress or parsley

- a twist of sliced lemon or orange peel speared with a toothpick with an olive on the end

- a slice of Kiwi fruit or melon

Row 2 — Soups

Chicken Yoghurt Soup

This unusual soup has been adapted from a Turkish recipe. Brown rice has been substituted for white rice for extra fibre, and mint added for refreshing flavour.

Ingredients

2 litres (4 pt) chicken stock

60 g (2 oz) brown rice

115 g (4 oz) minced raw chicken

250 ml (½ pt) low-fat yoghurt

black pepper

2 sprigs mint, freshly chopped

2 tablespoons parsley, chopped

Method

- Bring chicken stock to boil.
- Add rice and cook 30 minutes until soft.
- Add minced chicken and cook a further 5 minutes.
- Remove from heat, stir in yoghurt, pepper, mint and parsley.
- Serve hot with crusty bread.

Fish Chowder

It may look like a soup but you'll need a fork to eat it! The stock and vegetables add to the delicate texture and flavour of the fish. What could be nicer than steaming bowls of this soup around the fire with friends on a cold winter's evening?

Ingredients

450 g (1 lb) fresh fish fillets (any firm, white fish)

500 ml (1 pt) chicken stock

2 rashers of lean bacon, chopped

1 large onion, chopped

1 dessertspoon polyunsaturated oil

2 large potatoes, washed and diced

1 teaspoon cornflour

250 ml (½ pt) low-fat milk

black pepper

½ teaspoon dried oregano

1 tablespoon parsley, chopped

Method

- Poach fish for 15 minutes in chicken stock. Remove and cool.
- Flake fish, removing all skin and bones.
- Fry bacon and onion in oil until golden brown.
- Add potatoes and stock and simmer until tender.
- Thicken with cornflour.
- Heat milk and add to stock mixture. Bring to boiling point.
- Add fish, pepper and oregano. Sprinkle with parsley.

Meatball Soup

This soup is a meal on its own and full of flavour to tempt the palate. The meatballs are not fried in the usual way but baked to reduce the fat content. Served with some crusty wholemeal bread, a little grated Parmesan or Romano cheese and some fresh fruit to follow, it makes a nourishing repast.

Ingredients

2 stock cubes and 3 litres (6 pt) water or 3 litres (6 pt) chicken stock

3 carrots, chopped

3 sticks celery, chopped

1 egg

450 g (1lb) minced topside

1 slice wholemeal bread, crumbled

1 cup small noodles

1 400 g (13 oz approximately) can unsalted tomatoes, mashed

parsley, chopped

Method

- Place stock cubes and water in a saucepan, add carrots and celery.
- Bring to boil and simmer gently.
- Mix egg, mince and breadcrumbs and make into small balls. Place on a greased oven tray and bake in oven at 200°C (400°F) for 30 minutes.
- While meatballs are cooking add noodles and tomatoes to stock mixture and boil for 15 minutes.
- Place meatballs in soup, sprinkle with parsley and serve.

Shrimp and Tomato Soup

The shrimps add an exotic touch to this tomato-based soup and the lemon wedges a piquant flavour.

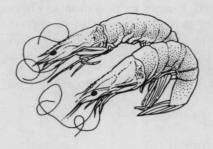

Ingredients

375 ml (¾ pt) good chicken stock

1 400 g (approximately 13 oz) can peeled, unsalted tomatoes, blended

1 tablespoon dehydrated tomato flakes

115 g (4 oz) peeled raw shrimps

125 ml (¼ pt) dry white wine

2 tablespoons chopped parsley

lemon wedges

Method

- Place chicken stock, tomatoes and tomato flakes in a saucepan and bring to the boil.
- Add shrimps and simmer for 2 minutes.
- Stir in white wine and sprinkle with parsley.
- Serve with lemon wedges.

Row 2 — Main Meals (Lunches and Dinners)

Baked Paprika Fish

Fish is rich in protein, vitamins and minerals and when cooked in this low-fat way is a nutritious dish. Served with a tossed salad and crunchy bread rolls it is perfect for those 'I don't feel like cooking' days.

Ingredients

1 fillet of fish per person (not too thick)

black pepper

paprika

lemon or lime slices

small knobs of margarine

Method

- Place fish fillets in an ovenproof dish and sprinkle with pepper and paprika.

- Place a slice of lemon or lime and a knob of margarine on each fillet.

- Cover with foil and bake in a moderate oven 190°C (375°F) for 12 minutes.

Chicken Cavendish Salad

This chicken salad is an exotic feast on a platter. The appetising combination of colour, flavour and texture makes it an ideal dish for a cold buffet luncheon or party. There is no limit to the variety of vegetables you can use to garnish the rice — be creative!

Salad Ingredients

1 medium-sized chicken

1 carrot, chopped

1 onion, chopped

1 ham steak, finely cubed

225 g (8 oz) cooked brown rice

2 eggs, hardboiled and cut lengthwise in quarters

baby tomatoes

green beans, cooked

Method

- Gently boil chicken with carrot and onion in enough water to cover, approximately ¾ hour.
- Chill chicken in liquid in which it is covered until it turns to a jelly.
- Remove chicken, retaining a little stock jelly.
- Shred chicken and combine with ham steak. Pile into the centre of a platter.
- Place rice in a ring around the outside.
- Garnish rice with eggs, tomatoes and beans.
- Pour dressing over and sprinkle top of chicken with chives or parsley.

Dressing Ingredients

2 tablespoons polyunsaturated oil

1 tablespoon lemon juice

black pepper

1 tablespoon walnuts, chopped

1 tablespoon raw onion, finely grated

Method

- Place all ingredients together in a screw-top jar and shake until well blended.

Chinese Spiced Chicken Wings

These chicken wings make excellent finger food or can be served with steamed or stir-fried vegetables. They are also delicious served cold with a salad. Don't forget to allow plenty of time to marinate them prior to cooking.

Ingredients

12 chicken wings

3 tablespoons dry sherry or white wine

2 tablespoons dark soy sauce

1 teaspoon five-spice powder

1 teaspoon grated green ginger

1 teaspoon honey

Method

- Make marinade by mixing together sherry, soy sauce, five-spice powder, ginger and honey.
- Place chicken wings in a flat casserole and pour marinade over.
- Refrigerate 3–4 hours, turning occasionally.
- Bake in a moderate oven for 35 minutes until nicely browned.

  or

- Grill, making sure you clip joints with a pair of kitchen scissors to prevent them curling up.

Greek Fish Fillets

This is an interesting and easy way to bake fish. It has more eye and taste appeal than fried fish and yet is much lower in fat.

Ingredients

4 fish fillets

juice of half a lemon

black pepper

1 small onion

1 teaspoon vegetable oil

1 tablespoon parsley, chopped

1 dessertspoon dehydrated tomato flakes

125 ml (¼ pt) dry white wine

1 large tomato, chopped

lemon peel, slivered

Method

- Place fish fillets in small, flat casserole dish and sprinkle with pepper and lemon juice.
- Cook onion in oil until transparent.
- Add parsley, tomato flakes, wine and tomato.
- Pour over fish.
- Arrange slivers of lemon peel on top.
- Bake approximately 30 minutes at 350°F (180°C).

Grilled Savoury Fish

Here's another quick, economical and tasty way to cook fish. The fresh herbs and cheese provide more than enough flavouring and give the fish a wonderful aroma. Steamed new potatoes and a green salad are the perfect accompaniment to this dish.

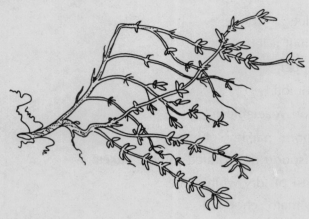

Ingredients

1 egg white, beaten until stiff

60 g (2 oz) tasty cheese, grated

fresh lemon thyme, oregano or tarragon, chopped

4 fish fillets

lemon slices

Method

- Fold grated cheese, herbs and pepper into beaten egg white.
- Lightly grill fish under medium heat on one side.
- Turn and spread with egg and cheese mixture.
- Grill until golden brown.
- Garnish with lemon slices.

Lamb with Orange

This is not your usual roast dripping with fat. The orange juice substitutes for the fat and keeps the meat moist and tangy-flavoured. Serve with potatoes baked in their jackets, whole steamed beans and Glazed Carrots (see page 78).

Ingredients

1 small leg lamb

grated rind 1 orange

1 teaspoon prepared mustard

black pepper

juice of 1 orange

125 ml (¼ pt) water

Method

- Remove fat from lamb
- Rub with orange peel, mustard and pepper and bake for 45 minutes in a moderate oven.
- Pour orange juice and water over lamb and finish roasting (another 30 minutes).
- Use pan juices thickened with a little cornflour to make gravy.

Meat Sauce for Pasta

It's not what's in pasta but what's done to it that makes it fattening. Add this sauce to your favourite pasta with a clear conscience as its flavour comes from a variety of low-fat ingredients.

Ingredients

2 onions, chopped

1 dessertspoon oil

450 g (1 lb) minced veal

1 400 g (approximately 13 oz) can peeled, unsalted tomatoes

2 tablespoons dehydrated tomato flakes

1 bay leaf

4 mushrooms, diced

250 ml (½ pt) red wine

black pepper

2 teaspoons dried oregano

Method

- Cook onions in oil until golden. Add veal, stirring until it browns lightly.
- Mash tomatoes, add to meat mixture with tomato flakes, bay leaf, mushrooms, red wine and black pepper.
- Bring to boil, reduce heat and simmer uncovered for 30 minutes or until most of the liquid has evaporated. Stir in oregano.

Mediterranean Baked Fish

This simple recipe turns ordinary fish fillets into an excuse for a celebration — but without the expense! The tomatoes give it an appetizing appearance, and only a tossed salad or lightly steamed vegetables are needed to complete a delicious meal.

Ingredients

2 large fish fillets

1 cup wholemeal breadcrumbs

1 tablespoon parsley, chopped

2 teaspoons grated lemon rind

3 teaspoons chopped fresh thyme (preferably lemon thyme)

black pepper

a little milk

2 large tomatoes, sliced

Method

- Wash, dry and trim the fish and place one fillet, skin side down, in an oiled, shallow, heat-proof dish.
- Make stuffing by combining breadcrumbs, parsley, lemon rind, thyme and pepper. Bind with a little milk.
- Cover the fish with the stuffing. Put the second fillet, skin side up, on top of the stuffing.
- Arrange tomato slices along the centre of the fish. Brush lightly with oil and bake, uncovered, in the centre of the oven at 190°C (375°F) for 40 minutes.
- Garnish with parsley.

Pickled Fish

This spicy fish dish has a wonderful aromatic flavour and is surprisingly simple to prepare. It is an adventure in taste and texture. Serve chilled in a marinade, it needs no embellishment except a crisp green salad. Bon appetit!

Ingredients

450 g (1 lb) white fish fillets cut into 2 cm (1 in) cubes

1 dessertspoon plain flour

black pepper

1 tablespoon polyunsaturated oil

1 medium onion, thinly sliced

1 dessertspoon curry powder

250 ml (½ pt) water

1 dessertspoon light brown sugar

1 dessertspoon grated fresh ginger root

2 bay leaves

125 ml (¼ pt) vinegar

2 cooking apples, peeled, cored and cubed

Method

- Sprinkle fish with flour and black pepper and place in a lightly oiled ovenproof dish.
- Heat oil in a saucepan, add onion and cook until transparent.
- Add curry powder, cook, stirring for 5 minutes.
- Add water, brown sugar, ginger, bay leaves, vinegar and apples and bring to boil, stirring constantly.
- Mix flour with a little water and add to marinade.
- Reduce heat and simmer uncovered for 10 minutes.

- Spoon marinade over fish, coating it evenly.
- Bake at 190°C (375°F) for 30 minutes.
- Cover with plastic wrap and marinate in refrigerator for 2 days before serving.
- Serve cold.

Salmon and Mushroom Sauce for Pasta

This subtle flavoured sauce is just right as a topping for pasta, rice or noodles. Served with some hot crusty bread and a side salad it makes a nutritious main meal.

Ingredients

1 tablespoon low-salt polyunsaturated margarine

6 small mushrooms, washed and sliced

1 tablespoon plain flour

375 ml (¾ pt) low-fat milk

60 g (2 oz) tasy cheese, grated

black pepper

1 220 g (approximately 7 oz) can pink salmon

½ tablespoon mixed fresh herbs, chopped

Method

- Melt margarine in a saucepan. Add mushrooms and cook for 3 minutes.
- Add flour and mix well. Cook until bubbling.
- Remove from heat and stir in milk, cheese and black pepper. Bring to boil, stirring constantly.
- Drain salmon and flake. Stir into sauce.
- Reheat and serve, sprinkled with herbs.

Satés with Peanut Sauce

This famous Indonesian dish makes a perfect party snack or main course. You can use veal, pork or chicken instead of steak for a change. The peanut sauce is very versatile — it doubles as a spread on sandwiches or with a little water added, can be used as a sauce for lightly steamed vegetables. This recipe makes four times the amount required. Freeze the rest for later use.

Saté Ingredients

450 g (1 lb) round or rump steak (lean)

2 tablespoons soy sauce

2 tablespoons white wine

1 heaped teaspoon coriander

1 heaped teaspoon ground aniseed

1 dessertspoon polyunsaturated vegetable oil

saté sticks

Method

- Cut steak into 2 cm (1 in) cubes.
- Mix soy sauce, wine, coriander, aniseed and oil well together.
- Soak steak overnight in marinade (or for at least 4 hours).
- Thread on saté sticks and grill or barbecue, turning once.
- Serve with Peanut Sauce, see over.

Peanut Sauce Ingredients

1 onion, finely chopped

1 teaspoon polyunsaturated oil

1 200 g (approximately 7 oz) jar unsalted crunchy peanut butter

250 ml (½ pt) water

juice of 1 lemon

60 g (2 oz) coconut

1 teaspoon soy sauce

¼ teaspoon chilli sauce

Method

- Cook chopped onion in oil.
- Add peanut butter, water, lemon juice, coconut, soy sauce and chilli sauce.
- Stir till well blended and simmer for 3 minutes.
- Add a little more water if necessary to obtain a creamy mixture.
- Serve hot or cold in a bowl, as an accompaniment to Satés.

Sesame Chicken

This is low-fat version of a favourite Middle Eastern dish. It has a wonderful nutty flavour and goes well with slices of tropical fruit or Tangy Apples (see page 126). Serve with rice and a fresh tossed salad.

Ingredients

2 tablespoons plain flour

1 teaspoon paprika

4 chicken pieces

1 egg

125 ml (¼ pt) water or milk

60 g (2 oz) sesame seeds

oil

Method

- Mix the flour and paprika together.
- Press chicken pieces into flour.
- Beat the egg with the water or milk and dip the chicken pieces into this liquid.
- Coat chicken pieces with sesame seeds.
- Place in a baking dish and brush lightly with oil.
- Bake in a moderate oven 190°C (375°F) for approximately 30 minutes or until sesame seeds are crisp and golden.

Turkey Noodle Casserole

This dish takes advantage of one of the many turkey products now available. It is a change from the usual roast turkey, and stays moist as it is steeped in a thick, flavoursome sauce.

Turkey Mixture Ingredients

450 g (1 lb) cooked wholemeal macaroni

1 dessertspoon polyunsaturated oil

2 onions, chopped

345 g (12 oz) turkey mince

1 teaspoon dried basil

Method

- Heat oil in a pan and gently fry onions until transparent.
- Add turkey mince and basil and cook, stirring constantly until just cooked — about 5 minutes.

Cheese Sauce Ingredients

1 tablespoon low-salt polyunsaturated margarine

1 tablespoon plain flour

500 ml (1 pt) low-fat milk

black pepper

90 g (3 oz) low-fat cheese, grated

fresh breadcrumbs

Method

- Melt margarine in a saucepan, stir in flour and cook 1 minute.
- Remove from heat, add milk and pepper and cook until thickened.
- Stir in cheese.
- Add turkey mixture to cheese sauce and stir cooked macaroni through.
- Place in a casserole, sprinkle top with fresh breadcrumbs and a little extra grated cheese.
- Bake in moderate oven 190°C (375°F) for 10–15 minutes.

Courgettes Stuffed with Veal

This delicious Greek dish shows you how to extend a small quantity of meat to make a main meal. For a vegetarian dish, replace the meat with a grain and seed combination such as rice and sunflower seeds or wheat and sesame seeds.

Ingredients

1 tablespoon polyunsaturated oil

1 onion, finely chopped

225 g (8 oz) minced veal

1 tomato, chopped

black pepper

1 teaspoon dried oregano

2 courgettes, approximately 20 cm (8 in) long

Method

- Heat oil in a saucepan and fry onion until transparent.
- Add minced veal and fry for 5 more minutes.
- Add tomatoes, pepper and oregano and cook for 10 minutes until meat is cooked.
- Bring water to the boil in a saucepan large enough to fit the courgettes. Boil courgettes for 5 minutes.
- Remove from heat. Cut in half lengthwise and scoop out the pulp. Chop finely and mix with meat mixture.
- Place filling mixture into courgette shells, and place in an ovenproof container.
- Cover courgettes with cheese sauce and bake in a moderate oven 190°C (375°F) for 20 minutes, or until top is lightly browned.

Cheese Sauce Ingredients

1 tablespoon low salt polyunsaturated margarine

1 tablespoon flour

375 ml (¾ pt) low-fat milk

90 g (3 oz) cheese, grated

Method

- Melt margarine in a saucepan.
- Add flour and stir until bubbling.
- Add milk and stir until boiling.
- Stir in cheese.

Row 2 — Dips, Spreads and Snacks

Crab Meat Dip

Crab meat makes an excellent low-fat dip for raw vegetable strips. Try it with a selection of well chilled young vegetables such as baby carrots, spring onions, broccoli and cauliflower florets.

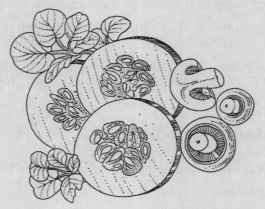

Ingredients

1 220 g (approximately 7 oz) can crab meat

250 ml (½ pt) low-fat natural yoghurt

1 tablespoon parsley, chopped

1 tablespoon chives, chopped

black pepper

Method

- Remove any shell from crab meat.
- Mix all ingredients together.
- Place in a bowl, chill and serve.

Cucumber and Yoghurt Dip

This refreshing dip originates from the Greek tzatziki. It's easy to make and can be served with crunchy vegetable fingers, Lebanese bread triangles (crisped in the oven) or as a cooling accompaniment to spicy Indian dishes. For variation try adding finely grated onion.

Ingredients

1 cucumber, finely diced

250 ml (½ pt) low-fat yoghurt

black pepper

clove garlic (optional)

1 tablespoon parsley, finely chopped

Method

- Mix together cucumber, yoghurt, pepper and finely crushed garlic.
- Place in a bowl and sprinkle with parsley.

Lazy Cheese Scones

The aroma of these scones as they come fresh from the oven will bring everyone into the kitchen. The shape is a bit unconventional, but the flavour is delightful. Try making them with all wholemeal flour for extra fibre or add some chopped fresh marjoram instead of parsley for a change. Served with a salad, they make an satisfying lunch-time meal.

Ingredients

225 g (8 oz) self-raising flour (half white, half wholemeal)

pinch cayenne pepper

1 tablespoon low-salt polyunsaturated margarine

115 g (4 oz) grated low-fat cheese

250 ml (½ pt) low-fat milk

1 egg

1 tablespoon parsley, chopped

sesame seeds

Method

- Sift flour and cayenne pepper.
- Rub margarine into flour.
- Add cheese.
- Mix milk, egg and parsley together and stir into flour mixture.
- Place a dessertspoon at a time on greased trays.
- Sprinkle with sesame seeds.
- Bake 10–12 minutes at 200°C (400°F).

Poppy Seed Turnovers

When you see how easy these little turnovers are to make, you'll wonder why you ever bought rolls. The poppy seeds give them a delicious nutty flavour and they are the perfect accompaniment to the soups in this book. This recipe makes approximately 20 turnovers and you can freeze any extra to be reheated later.

Ingredients

90 g (3 oz) low-salt polyunsaturated margarine

1 egg

450 g (1 lb) self-raising flour (half wholemeal, half white)

250 ml (½ pt) low-fat milk

poppy seeds

Method

- Beat margarine until soft.
- Add egg and beat well.
- Fold in flour alternately with milk, mixing to a soft dough.
- Turn on to a lightly floured board, knead lightly.
- Roll out to 1 cm (½ in) thickness.
- Cut into circles approximately 6 cm (2½ in) in diameter.
- Brush half of each round with milk and fold over, pressing edges lightly together.
- Brush tops lightly with milk and sprinkle with poppy seeds.
- Place on a greased oven tray and bake in a hot oven 200°C (400°F) for 10–12 minutes.
- Split and serve hot with a little margarine.

Ricotta and Tomato Dip

This wonderful dip is particularly good with vegetable straws or fingers of wholemeal toast. It also substitutes for butter or other fat spreads on bread or crispbreads. Remember to only make as much as you need as the low-fat content of ricotta means that it cannot be frozen.

Ingredients

225 g (8 oz) ricotta cheese

1 tomato, diced into small pieces

1 spring onion, chopped

4 black olives, pitted and chopped

1 tablespoon parsley, chopped

paprika

Method

- Mash ricotta cheese in a bowl.
- Add tomato, onion, olives and parsley and lightly stir.
- Place in a serving bowl and sprinkle with paprika.

164

Salmon Spread

This tasty, low-fat spread is delicious either as a sandwich filling with cucumber, bean sprouts or lettuce, or as a dip served with crisp vegetable straws or toasted wholemeal Lebanese bread triangles. You can use lime instead of lemon for extra tanginess.

Ingredients

220 g (8 oz) fresh ricotta cheese

220 g (approximately 7 oz) can pink salmon, drained with bones removed.

1 dessertspoon lemon juice

1 dessertspoon grated lemon rind

black pepper

1 tablespoon finely chopped chives

Method

- Beat cheese, salmon, lemon juice and lemon rind.
- Stir in chives.
- Decorate with a twist of lemon when serving as a dip.

4
More About Food and Nutrition

Introduction

This chapter is an alphabetical list of useful pointers which build on the ideas in the three previous chapters and also focus on some specific food and nutrition issues which may be of concern to you. Each topic begins with a short statement on the appropriate action to take for long-term health and the reasons why.

As you can imagine, a great deal of painstaking research is required to produce answers to questions about the specific steps to take to keep healthy and free from disease. There is not space in this chapter to discuss the enormous amount of research that has been conducted, and debates on how experimental findings should be interpreted. Volumes have been written on each topic. The aim here is to provide some general guidelines to follow that may whet your appetite to read more detailed information.

It is not easy to change well-entrenched eating patterns and incorporate new recipes into your repertoire. Trial and analysis is required before you can persuade your taste buds that the new dishes are to their liking. It's probably worth spending some time mulling over the ideas in this chapter before trying the recipes in the previous one. A little thought now could pay handsome dividends later. The more you feel a winner with your first cooking forays, the more likely you are to pursue the adventure.

Don't expect immediate inspiration or instant results. New ideas have to be worked on, blended, kneaded, a pinch of a notion here, a sprinkle of a thought there. But the products will be so crisp, colourful and creative that you'll amaze yourself — and your friends.

Appetite Regulation

Action to take:
Keep up a good appetite through regular exercise.

- The more we exercise the more we eat.
- The more we eat the more likely we are to be well nourished — **provided** that the extra food is chosen from Rows 1 and 2 of the Healthy Diet Triangle. Extra food from Rows 3 and 4 leads to problems associated with high fat and sugar intakes.
- A consistently small appetite, associated with a lack of exercise, coupled with eating foods from Rows 3 and 4, leads to a risk of not taking in enough essential nutrients and dietary fibre.

Relationship between Energy Input and Output

The amount of food we eat is determined by the amount of exercise we take. This is easy enough to say but, as you can imagine, it has taken a great deal of research to establish this fact. It is technically very difficult to measure accurately energy input and output over a period of weeks. There have been a number of such studies carried out with soldiers. Why soldiers? Because they can be ordered to undertake particular activities over extended periods of time and what they eat can be very closely monitored. And they can be court-marshalled if they try to sneak an illicit bar of chocolate!

Appetite does not necessarily reflect the amount of exercise we do each day. We may be too tired to eat after strenuous activity. The studies with soldiers show that strenuous exercise tends to stimulate a hearty appetite one or two days later. Furthermore, when measurements are carried out over a week to ten days there is a close correspondence between the amount of energy expended and the amount of energy consumed.

What Controls our Appetite?

There is a centre in the brain which controls our appetite through monitoring:

- the rate glucose disappears from the blood stream as it enters the cells of muscles and all other body tissues to drive their activities.
- changes in energy stores as body fat is drawn upon to meet the body's need for fuel.

We feel hungry when the appetite centre registers that fuel reserves have been depleted below a certain level. The depletion rate of these body reserves of fuel depends on how fast they are used for activities such as pumping the heart and muscle movement. The more vigorous and extended the activities we undertake, the more rapidly glucose and fat stores are used and the more hungry we feel — although not necessarily immediately after the activity.

Many of us think we are hungry, when the clock reaches the time we usually eat. Even so the amount of food energy we consume in the course of a week, for example, is closely related to the amount of exercise we do during that time.

Calcium

It used to be thought that we outgrew our need for milk and other calcium rich-foods once we became adults. There is now firm scientific evidence that calcium is important in later life in preventing the development of osteoporosis, particularly in post-menopausal women.

Many women and some men face a future in which they will fall victim to the painful and depressing disease called osteoporosis. This disease is a weakening of the bones which shows up in later life. Women suffer wrist fractures in their 50s, spine fractures in their 60s and hip fractures in their 70s.

Oestrogen therapy is probably the most widely used method

169

of preventing the development of this condition.

At present the role of calcium is the subject of a great deal of research and public interest. There is now strong evidence to suggest that calcium prevents or at least slows down the loss of bone material. It has been found that boosting calcium intake at the time of menopause and in succeeding years can substantially reduce the rate or bone tissue loss which may prevent the development of brittle bones later in life.

There is controversy about the value of calcium supplements because of possible dangerous side effects. Excess calcium can lead to kidney stones, particularly when there is a personal or family history of this disorder.

Action to take:

Maintain an intake of at least 1000 mg of calcium per day by drinking milk and eating foods such as low-fat cheeses and yoghurt.

- Keep up an adequate calcium intake to maintain independence and agility in later life.
- The majority view of researchers in this field is that the recommended amount of calcium should be consumed from food sources rather than supplements. The chart of calcium-rich foods will show you how to get an adequate intake.
- Increase the amounts you use of milk and other dairy foods, preferably those low in fat, as your main strategy to boost calcium intakes. If you have problems digesting milk try lactose-reduced milk, in addition to yoghurt and cheeses.

People at Risk

People most likely to develop brittle and fragile bones are:

- Those who have a family history of the condition.
- Small and slim people who have small frames with a low bone mass.
- Those who undertook a number of 'crash diets' when they were younger, as weight loss is accompanied by bone loss.
- Those who do very little exercise.
- Smokers.
- Those who have high levels of alcohol, coffee and salt in their diet.

170

Sources of Dietary Calcium

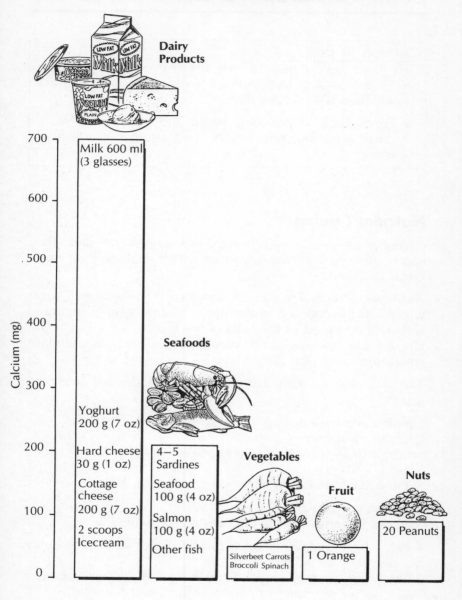

Dairy Products

Seafoods

Vegetables

Fruit

Nuts

Calcium (mg)

700
600
500
400
300
200
100
0

Milk 600 ml (3 glasses)

Yoghurt 200 g (7 oz)

Hard cheese 30 g (1 oz)

Cottage cheese 200 g (7 oz)

2 scoops Icecream

4–5 Sardines

Seafood 100 g (4 oz)

Salmon 100 g (4 oz)

Other fish

Silverbeet Carrots Broccoli Spinach

1 Orange

20 Peanuts

Complex Carbohydrates

Action to take:

Try to ensure that most of your dietary energy comes from foods which contain complex carbohydrates — starch in association with dietary fibre.

- Foods such as potatoes, bread and other grain products, and legumes are the best sources of dietary energy.

Nutrient Content

Carbohydrates are a major source of energy in the diet. They can be divided into two categories which relate to their nutritional functions:

- Available or digestible carbohydrates such as starch and sugar which can be digested in the upper gastrointestinal tract and absorbed and used in the cells of the body.
- Unavailable or indigestible carbohydrates such as cellulose which form part of dietary fibre.

The available carbohydrates can also be divided into two groups:

Simple carbohydrates
- Glucose (dextrose) in grapes.
- Fructose (fruit sugar) in figs and honey.
- Lactose (milk sugar).
- Sucrose (table sugar) in sugar cane and sugar beet.

Complex carbohydrates
- Starches in cereal grains, potatoes and legumes.

Foods which contain complex carbohydrates tend to be bulky because they contain:
- Fibre — for example, in wholegrain cereals and vegetables.
- Water — for example, in potatoes, fruits and porridge.

Foods which are rich in complex carbohydrates generally contain protein, vitamins and minerals.

172

Sugar

Sugar is blamed as the culprit in a wide range of ills — from heart disease and diabetes to deviant behaviour — none of which has been proved. The evidence shows that the only finger that can be pointed at sugar is that it causes dental caries. Many people find that their problem of overweight is exacerbated by sweet foods. This is because the availability of sweet foods tempts them to eat more kilojoules than they need.

The presence of sugar used in manufactured foods can readily be tasted in soft drinks and cordials, confectionery, breakfast cereals and fruit products. It is less easy to detect in, for example, some soups, canned vegetables, sauces and salad dressings.

If you want to lose weight reduce the amount of sugar you eat. Easier said than done? It actually isn't hard if it is part of your overall strategy to modify your dietary and exercise patterns.

Ways to reduce sugar in the diet:

- Use less of all sugars including white, brown, and raw as well as honey and syrups.
- Eat fresh fruit or canned unsweetened fruit instead of cakes, icecream, sweet biscuits and sugary desserts.
- Read food labels for clues on sugar content.
- Substitute other flavours for the sweet taste of sugar in fruit desserts — unsweetened citrus, mango or apple juice, orange flower water or rosewater, cinnamon or cloves, freshly ground ginger.
- Use artificial sweeteners as a first step to break away from habitual use of sugar — but phase these out too.

Flours

Wholemeal flours made from cereal grains are good sources of starch, protein, B vitamins and fibre. Use wholemeal instead of white flour in cooking where possible. Wholemeal flour contains the whole of the wheat grain including the bran and wheat germ.

Bread made from 100-per-cent extraction, wholewheat or whole rye flour contains the most fibre. Danish sandwiches

173

made from wholemeal bread and low-fat toppings (see recipes Chapter 3) make a substantial snack 'on the run.'

Pasta

There's more to pasta than spaghetti and meatballs! Nutrition-wise cooks have given pasta a new found reputation as a thoroughly wholesome food. Served with a low-fat meat, fish, vegetable or herb topping, it makes a substantial, yet healthy meal. Remember to cook it until *al dente* and serve immediately. Try some of the low-fat sauces listed in the recipes in Chapter 3.

Pasta is made from a hard wheat called durum which does not rise during baking and is therefore unsuitable for making bread and cakes. Apart from the wide variety of pasta shapes, each blessed with its own Italian name, there are both the dried and fresh versions in white, green (spinach), pink (tomato) and wholemeal. The fresh pasta is available from speciality food shops and has a superior taste and texture. The wholemeal pasta takes longer to cook than other versions and is heavier in texture.

Pasta is a moderate source of protein and calcium and is low in fat. There are some high-protein varieties on the market which have some of the wheat flour replaced with high-protein soya flour.

Legumes — Beans and Peas

Legumes are an excellent source of vegetable protein and the basis of vegetarian diets. They also contain starch, fibre, B vitamins, iron and calcium.

Dried legumes (pulses) include a wide variety of dried beans and peas and form the basis of many Greek and Indian dishes. They have now found their way into Western cooking because they are so versatile, inexpensive and nutritious. Although pulses generally require soaking before cooking, the effort is well worth it.

They can be a substitute for meat in vegetarian dishes such as soya bean casseroles and tacos, used to extend meat and vegetable dishes, soups and casseroles, added to salads or used to make dips and spreads such as hoummus.

174

Cooking Instructions

Bean or Pea	Soak in cold water	Simmer in saucepan, covered with water	Pressure Cooker
Lentils		30 minutes	10 minutes
Backeyed beans		35 minutes	10 minutes
Mung, aduki		30–60 minutes	5–10 minutes
Chick peas	4–5 hours	3–4 hours	30 minutes
Brown beans	4–5 hours	3–4 hours	30 minutes
Borlotti beans	4–5 hours	3–4 hours	30 minutes
Butter beans	4–5 hours	3–4 hours	10–20 minutes
Kidney beans	4–5 hours	1–2 hours	15–20 minutes
Haricot beans	4–5 hours	1–2 hours	15–20 minutes
Soya beans	overnight	3–4 hours	15–20 minutes
Broad beans	overnight	4–5 hours	30 minutes
Lima beans	overnight	2–3 hours	30 minutes
Soya grits		10–15 minutes	

Potatoes

Potatoes (without added fat) are low in energy density because they are mainly made up of starch and water (75 to 80 per cent water). They contain small amounts of minerals and B vitamins, and can also contribute useful quantities of vitamin C.

Sweet potatoes (without added fat) have a third more calories and slightly less protein than white potatoes. They are rich sources of vitamin A and contain more calcium and iron than white potatoes.

The blame for the 'fattening' qualities of the much-maligned potato is the fat that so often goes with it — when it is fried in oil, roasted in meat fat, stuffed with cheese or sautéd in butter. Potatoes are a nutritious, non-fattening vegetable when steamed or baked in their skins for extra fibre and flavoured with herbs, spices or cottage cheese instead of oil and fat.

Nuts and Seeds

Nuts and seeds are good sources of fibre, vitamins and minerals. However, they are high in fat and hence calories. Used sparingly they can boost the crunchy texture of food.

Nuts and seeds are delicious added to a wide variety of dishes. For example:

- Slivered almonds in steamed vegetables.
- Peanuts in curries.
- Sesame or poppy seeds in a crunchy topping for bread and buns.
- Sunflower and pumpkin seeds in muesli, salads and muffins.

Cooking Methods

Action to take:
Use the cooking method that will enhance the flavour and texture of a particular food and, at the same time, does not require the addition of fat, salt or sugar.

- Experiment — with vegetables for example — try a variety of cooking methods such as stir-frying or barbecuing in foil instead of boiling or steaming.

Boiling

Uses:
- Tougher cuts of meat, chicken, vegetables, rice, pasta.
  Advantages:
- Quick, easy, clean.
- Food remains moist.
  Hints:
- Use a minimum of water.
- Cook until just done.
- Use cooking water for soups, stocks and sauces.
- Vegetables:
  Leave whole if possible.
  Add as soon as water has boiled.
  Remove when cooked to avoid loss of nutrients.

Stir-Frying

Uses:
- Vegetables, chicken fillets, seafood.

Advantages:
- Quick and easy.
- Preserves a high percentage of nutrients, colour, flavour and texture.

Hints:
- Use a wok or deep-sided frying pan.
- All ingredients need to be prepared and on hand as cooking process only takes a few minutes.
- Cut vegetables into evenly-sized pieces so they will cook in same amount of time.
- Cook vegetables in correct order — ones that need longest cooking time first, onions for example.
- Turn rather than stir food constantly.
- Use special turning utensil with curved bottom available from Asian grocery shops to fit wok base.
- Add touches of sherry, soy sauce, stock, cornflower and ginger at end of cooking time for additional flavour and moisture.

Dry-Frying

Uses:
- Tender cuts of meat, chicken, fish, eggs, pancakes and vegetables such as mushrooms, eggplant, tomatoes and onions.

Advantages:
- Only needs a smear of oil.

Hints:
- Heat pan before brushing a little oil over the base.
- Dip meat, chicken or fish in egg and breadcrumbs, wholemeal flour, finely chopped nuts or sesame seeds for a crunchy coating.
- A non-stick frying pan is ideal for this method.

Steaming

Uses:
- Vegetables, chicken, fish, rice.

Advantages:
- Greater retention of colour, flavour and nutrient content than boiling.

- Requires no fat during cooking process.
  Hints:
- Boil water before cooking vegetables in steamer.
- Keep water boiling during cooking process, adding more when necessary.
- For effect — use a Chinese bamboo steamer which can be brought straight to the table.

Grilling

Uses:
- Tender cuts of meat, hamburgers, chicken pieces, oily fish fillets, fruit and vegetables such as mushrooms, tomatoes, eggplant, pineapple and bananas, and toasted cheese slices.
  Advantages:
- Quick cooking method which drains fat.
  Hints:
- Preheat griller on high setting, then place food underneath and turn heat down to complete cooking.

Casseroling and Stewing

Uses:
- Tougher cuts of meat, poultry, fish, vegetarian dishes.
  Advantages:
- Slow cooking which requires very little supervision during cooking process.
- Cooked food can be refrigerated for 1–2 days or frozen for later use.
- Fat can be skimmed off once dish has cooled.
- Minerals and vitamins which have leached out of food during cooking process are retained in sauce.
  Hints:
- Trim all visible fat off meat, and skin off poultry.
- Add wine and herbs for extra flavour.
- Casseroles — cook in oven in a covered ovenproof dish.
- Stews — cook on top of stove in a heavy pot with lid.

Oven Cooking (Roasting)

Uses:
- Joints of meat, whole chicken, turkey, duck, chicken or fish fillets in foil, whole vegetables, such as potatoes, pumpkin.

Advantages:
- Slow cooking requires very little supervision during cooking process.
- Food cooked whole retains its shape and has visual appeal.
Hints:
- Roasting meat.
    Preheat oven to 210°C (425°F) and cook for 20 minutes to seal in juices.
    Reduce temperature to 190°C (375°F) for remaining cooking time.
    Roast meat on rack so fat drips away.
    Cover meat in foil to prevent outside becoming tough.
    Remove foil and baste meat for remaining 30 minutes of cooking time.

Barbecuing

Uses:
- Tender cuts of meat, satés or kebabs, fish, poultry, corn on cob, vegetables or fruit in foil, such as potatoes, carrots, bananas.
Advantages:
- Seals in flavour.
- Fat drips away.
Hints:
- Use an open grill rather than a heavy plate to avoid frying food.
- Add food when flames have died down to glowing coals.
- Use a spray of water if flames flare up during cooking.

Microwave

Uses:
- Melting — margarine, cheese.
- Boiling — water, drinks, soups.
- Roasting — poultry, meat, fish.
- Sautéing — meat, vegetables.
- Baking — muffins, cakes, breads, scones.
- Drying — herbs, bread, fruit.
- Steaming — fish, vegetables.
- Poaching — fish, eggs.
- Heating — cold dishes.
- Thawing — frozen foods.

179

Advantages:
- Cooks or defrosts food quickly with very little loss of nutrients.
- Cooking time reduced by up to 75 per cent.
- Shape and colour retained.
- Cooked and served in same container.
Hints:
- Cook dry or with a minimum amount of water depending on food.

Pressure Cooking

Uses:
- Soups, dried legumes, stews, vegetables.
Advantages:
- Reduces cooking time to approximately one-third of normal stove top cooking.
Hints:
- Some recommended cooking times.
    stew — 20 minutes.
    potatoes — 5 minutes.
    carrots — 4 minutes.
- Read your instructions carefully.

Diet and Cancer

Action to take:
Eat a low-fat, high-fibre diet according to the dietary guidelines in this book.

- This recommendation is in accord with statements published by several authoritative bodies, such as the American Cancer Society and the National Academy of Sciences in the United States. However, it does not imply that this dietary pattern *will* prevent the development of cancer. There is not sufficient evidence for firm scientific pronouncements to be made about associations between diet and cancer.
- Indirect evidence does indicate that a diet based largely on Healthy Diet Triangle Row 1 and Row 2 foods could lessen the risk of suffering from particular forms of cancer such as cancer of the large intestine (including colon and rectum) and breast.

Epidemiological Studies on Cancer

The search for the causes of cancer has been an important branch of cancer research. A great deal of effort has been devoted to studying the influence of both environmental and genetic factors in the incidence of this disease. In the course of this research it has become clear that most cancers have external causes and, *in principle*, should therefore be preventable. In other words cancer can now be seen to be just another of the preventable diseases — perhaps just as preventable at the end of the twentieth century as were the infectious diseases at the end of the last century.

It is possible to estimate the contribution that various factors might have on the occurrence of cancer. Among these are:

- Diet.
- Smoking.
- Radiation.
- Occupation.
- Infective agents such as viruses.
- Hormones.
- Drugs.

The leading researcher in the field, Sir Richard Doll, has estimated that diet is the main environmental factor to which cancer can be linked. He estimates that if alcohol is included, approximately 40 per cent of cancer deaths in the United States can be attributable to diet.

As yet there is not sufficient evidence to show which dietary components predispose or prevent various forms of cancer and how. The evidence that is available is the subject of fierce debates between various researchers in the field.

Present Indications on Relationship between Dietary Factors and Cancer

A dietary pattern which is high in dietary fibre from cereal grains, contains plenty of fruits and vegetables (green and yellow) and is low in fat, cholesterol and alcohol seems protective against cancer of the large bowel, breast and prostate. The reasons for this are not yet known but are the subject of intense research.

The nature of possible active cancer-preventing components in vegetables and fruits is the subject of current research. One likely substance is beta-carotene, found widely in green and yellow plant foods and which is converted into vitamin A in the body. The results of several substantial trials currently under way should provide clearer answers, in the next few years, on whether beta-carotene does protect against the development of cancer.

There is little evidence to date of a link between food additives and cancer, according to Sir Richard Doll. Furthermore, there does not appear to be protective value from vitamin supplements unless the diet lacks the normal recommended amounts.

We can only hope that further rigorous research and evaluation in the next few years brings us closer to a firm basis for formulating guidelines on how to prevent cancer.

Energy Considerations

The Meaning of the Term 'Energy'

The statement that carbohydrate and fat supply energy in the diet means that they provide the driving force for the body's chemical reactions, including those which produce muscle movement. This 'capacity to do work' of a food is measured in calories or kilojoules (1 calorie = 4.2 kilojoules).

The scientific use of the term 'energy' does not have the same meaning as that used in food advertisements. For example, a sales pitch for some sweets and drinks is that they give you 'quick energy'. The message suggests that they will invigorate you when you have mid-morning, mid-afternoon or evening doldrums, because your low blood sugar is making you sag and all you need is a little sweet spurt to get you going again.

The promise of instant energy is a fallacy. The body maintains a small but adequate carbohydrate storage depot to call upon when energy output demands it. It is called glycogen and is stored in the liver and in the muscles. It can be quickly converted to glucose when the body needs more blood sugar. A car will not perform any better if the petrol in the tank is topped up, nor will our bodies if the glycogen stores are topped up after eating sweets.

Energy Density

This is the amount of energy in a food per gram of food. It is measured in a bomb calorimeter and the units are calories or kilojoules per gram.

Which has the highest energy density, carbohydrate or fat? In other words, which has the greater amount of kilojoules per gram? Look at the table below for the answer.

Energy Density

Component	Calories per gram	Kilojoules per gram
Protein	4	17
Carbohydrate	4	16
Fat	9	37

Does this surprise you?

Many people think that carbohydrate has the highest energy density but you can see that this is not the case. The concentration of energy in fat is the highest and is about 2.25 times greater than carbohydrate and protein.

Significance of Energy Density in Weight Control

The more fat a food contains the higher will be its energy density. For example, look at how the energy content of one medium-sized potato varies according to the way it is cooked.

	Calories	Kilojoules
Baked or boiled	70	294
Mashed with milk	80	336
Mashed with milk and 1 teaspoon butter	115	483
Baked in fat or oil	200	840
Made into chips	350	1470

Does this help you to appreciate that the fattening properties of potatoes are not in the potatoes themselves but in how they are cooked?

The energy density of foods is influenced by fat content as well as by fibre and water content. For example, fruit and cake both contain sugar (16 kilojoules or 4 calories per gram) but their energy densities differ considerably because fruit has a much highter water and fibre content. A large apple weighing 225 grams (7 ounces) has 567 kilojoules (135 calories) whereas a plain donut has 3360 kilojoules (800 calories)!

It's easy to see that fruit, which contains complex carbohydrate and is bulky food, would produce a feeling of fullness more quickly than the cake. Therefore, we are more likely to consume fewer kilojoules on a diet with plenty of fruit than one which is high in cakes and sweet desserts.

Exercise

Action to take:
Regular daily exercise!

- We can maintain a positive response to challenges and invitations when we feel physically fit. 'Yes, I can manage that' and 'Yes, I would love to come.'
- Ask yourself 'What kind of physical activity would best fit into the way I want to live in the future?' rather than 'Should I do some regular exercise?'
- Only undertake exercise you enjoy otherwise you won't persist. You might not enjoy it immediately — but after a few small triumphs, you'll be off and running, or walking, or swimming.

Why Should we Exercise in the Vital Years?

Keeping to a pattern of regular exercise is not easy. There are so many distractions that get in the way of our walk or swim. It's hard to get back into a regular pattern of exercise if we've let our daily physical activity slip.

Yet this is precisely what is required to remain healthy. There is now persuasive scientific evidence to show that activities which get the heart pumping at a higher rate than usual and stretch our muscles are critical to maintain physical and mental well-being. Physical exercise lifts the spirit, keeps us fit for the tasks we set ourselves and helps prevent or reduce the effects of heart disease, obesity and diabetes.

People in older age groups can benefit from exercise just as much as the young. This has been demonstrated by laboratory studies and feedback from people who take up 'keep-fit' activities of various kinds in later life. Renewed vigour can be regained to a remarkable extent at any age through regular exercise. These findings show that physical inactivity, with accompanying stiffness in the joints, occasional loss of balance, breathlessness and fatigue, have much more to do with low personal aspirations than physical deterioration. And interestingly, it seems that the ones who are most likely to give away 'keeping going' are those who feel they have reached a stage in their lives when they *deserve* a rest. A most unfortunate perception!

Over-protective friends and relatives can put you off exercise by pointing out the dangers. Rest assured, the dangers have been unduly emphasised. The benefits are too great to dismiss. It's worth having a discussion about this with your doctor and perhaps also with a fitness instructor at your local leisure centre or branch of the National Heart Foundation.

Here are some suggestions for recreational exercises you can do on your own — although all of these can be done in company too — or which require the participation of others. You might enjoy mixing and matching one or two of both kinds of exercise — and gain extra health benefits too.

Solo Exercises

- Walking — the way to see your own neighbourhood and further afield from pavement level. You could be amazed at what this view can reveal and who knows what interesting people you might meet *en route*. Walking builds and maintains stamina. A pair of shoes with thick soles and no heels is a good investment.

- Swimming — a very useful exercise to keep supple and to regain both strength and stamina. You can also expend a substantial number of kilojoules if you keep up a fast pace or swim a long distance. At a more leisurely pace you can set targets for yourself. If you complete a certain number of laps this could give you a sense of achievement and a boost to your self esteem. If you're thinking of taking up swimming for the first time — and lots of people do so very successfully when they're in the middle years — it's a good idea to have a few lessons from a professional coach.

- Cycling — a way to explore further afield along new byways, catch the breeze and push yourself along at a pace which is moderately hard but not difficult. A few uphill climbs can do wonders for the 'ticker'.
- Callisthenics — for strength, mobility and flexibility. The name itself conjures up images of tortuous, grunt-and-groan-filled pain. It's not like that at all if you set about it with some clear guidelines in mind. For a start it only needs to be done for 10 minutes each day, which is quite feasible in anybody's schedule, and in a way which just keeps you stretched.
- Jogging — for stalwarts! An excellent activity to keep the heart in good order. It's a form of exercise that has become popular in recent years, and there's a lot of fun in both training and participating in fun runs. Don't ever feel that jogging is a 'must'. It's not.

Exercise with Others

A local leisure centre may provide the facilities and programmes for activities you enjoy.

Bushwalking is a social activity which might take your fancy. Or you could take the opportunity to take up a sport such as golf, tennis, bowls or bowling.

You could also try exercises set to music — Jane Fonda-style. Aerobic dancing and jazz ballet are vigorous forms of exercise set to music but something more leisurely might suit you better. It's amazing to hear how many people enjoy recreational gymnastics who previously would have classified themselves as real layabouts.

Participate in a group activity and it could set you on a track to:

- Renewed vigour and zest for living.
- Friendships with like minded people.
- Escape from 'rustout'. (See page 28.)

Fish

Fish is regarded as a valuable component of a healthy-heart diet, because it is low both in cholesterol and in fat. Fat that is present in fish contains a much higher proportion of polyunsaturated fatty acids than the fat in other animal foods such as meat, butter, eggs or milk.

Furthermore, some of the fatty acids in fish (called omega-3s) are two to five times more potent in lowering blood cholesterol than vegetable oils. These fatty acids also make the blood slower to clot. They also suppress the development of lesions which lead to narrowing of the arteries, particularly those that carry blood to the heart itself.

Some health authorities go so far as to recommend that fish should be put above all other foods in the diet for preventing heart disease.

How much Fish should I eat to Obtain this Protection?

Dutch investigators studied the relationship between fish consumption and coronary heart disease in Zutphen, Holland. Information about fish consumption by 852 men without heart disease was collected in 1960 and followed up for 20 years. This research showed that middle-aged men who ate, on average, between 1 and 29 grams (1 ounce) of fish per day had a death rate which was 40 per cent lower than that of those who ate no fish at all. Eating more than an average of 30 grams (1 ounce) per day was associated with 60 per cent reduction. These findings were independent of other risk factors such as body fat, physical activity, blood pressure and cigarette smoking.

In practical terms at least one, and preferably two, fish dishes should be eaten each week. There are a number of delicious fish dishes in Chapter 3 which you might like to try.

Relief from Arthritis

These same omega-3 fatty acids are now known to have a protective influence on the substances in blood which lead to the body's immune system attacking its own tissues, as happens in rheumatoid arthritis and lupus erythematosus. Evidence for this protective effect has so far been obtained mainly from experiments with animals but it is likely that the results of trials on humans will be reported during the next year or two.

The Value of Fish Oil Supplements

Supplements containing fish-oil concentrates are now being

heavily promoted. There is no general agreement among researchers in the field about their value, mainly because much still needs to be learned about the dietary levels of the omega-3 fatty acids required to achieve particular effects. Some experts consider that eating fish twice a week will achieve the same benefits as taking fish oil supplements. Others suggest that a more concentrated source of fish oil in the form of supplements is necessary to achieve benefits such as the prevention of heart disease.

There's no doubt we'll hear a lot more about this issue. There is a great deal of research under way on the significance of fish and fish products in the diet of people in their vital years.

Action to take:
Eat at least one fish dish per week and preferably two.

- There is now strong evidence that eating fish provides protection against heart disease.
- There is suggestive evidence that it also helps in the management of arthritis.

Fish has always been an integral part of a balanced diet. It is an excellent source of vitamins, minerals and protein and, in most species, is low in fat. These properties make fish a valuable part of a weight control diet.

Food Additives

All food additives in commercial use have been accepted as safe by the Australian National Health and Medical Research Council and can only be used in specified foods and in approved amounts. Furthermore, we are unlikely to be harmed by the presence of additives in processed foods if our diet is made up mainly of fresh foods and is in accord with Rows 1 and 2 of the Healthy Diet Triangle.

Recently Sir Richard Doll, who 20 years ago led research which first linked cigarette smoking with lung cancer, and who has subsequently studied other environmental influences on cancer, has reported that there is no evidence that food additives lead to cancer in humans. He suggests that the use of preservatives in place of salt-pickling may well be responsible for the declining incidence of stomach cancer.

There is no evidence for the claim of an allergy or hyperactivity epidemic from the consumption of food additives.

Action to take:

Use fresh foods as the bulk of your daily diet complemented by selected processed and convenience foods.

- Many of us have doubts about the synthetic chemicals added to processed foods because we feel manipulated and not in control of what we eat. We can do our own manipulating by mixing fresh with processed foods to add variety to our diet. This action will minimise any risk from harm from exposure to particular additives.
- It is a fallacy that all natural ingredients are good for us and those that are created through science and technology are bad for us.

Sensitivity to Food Additives

There is evidence that a small proportion of the population react to specific food additives like sulphur dioxide, tartrazine and monosodium glutamate. The new method of listing additives on packaged-food labels — the general class name and a three digit number — is now in operation and makes them easy to identify. The list is readily available from health professionals.

The Technical Need for Additives

Most processed foods contain additives — substances added for a specific technical purpose such as to improve appearance, texture, flavour, keeping-quality or nutritional value.

The use of preservatives extends the range of foods available at all times of the year and reduces the danger of microbiological contamination.

Food Labelling

The starting point is to focus on selecting foods from Rows 1 and 2 from the Healthy Diet Triangle and products derived

189

from these foods, such as wholemeal flour. The name of the food has to indicate the main ingredients and musn't be misleading.

Next, look for the presence of other ingredients which are of interest to you, such as salt if you want to limit the amount of sodium you eat. The label will give you part of the information you require. When a food contains more than one ingredient an appropriate designation of each must be given in a list, setting out the ingredients in the order of the amounts present in the food. This applies to all packaged foods except alcoholic beverages, most cheeses, essences and soft drinks in unlabelled glass bottles.

The listing of ingredients in order of abundance doesn't tell you what proportion of the food is made up by each ingredient. When sugar, for example, is listed as the third ingredient it could comprise 30 or 3 per cent of the food.

Food additives have to be included in the list of ingredients by their class name, such as 'preservative' or 'colour' and specific additives must be identified by their code number. (See Food Additives, page 188.)

Sweeteners come in various forms — and disguises! For a start, table sugar (sucrose) may be only one of several sugars listed on the label. Others may also be present and these are listed separately — fructose, dextrose, lactose, maltose, corn syrup. The total amount of sugar can exceed 40 per cent of some breakfast cereals. 'No added sugar' means only that no extra *sucrose* has been added during processing.

If you want to reduce your sugar intake to reduce kilojoules, beware of foods which contain several different sugars or sugar substitutes such as sorbitol or mannitol, which all have similar kilojoule contents.

The artificial sweeteners — saccharin, aspartame and cyclamates — do not contribute significant dietary energy and are permitted in 'low-kilojoule foods'. These sweeteners should be listed by name.

Fat, too, appears in different forms such as oil, shortening, margarine and animal fats. A fat or oil labelled 'polyunsaturated' must have at least twice as much polyunsaturated fatty acids as saturated and its cholesterol content must be stated on the label.

Salt is found in significant amounts in foods such as baking powder, dried soups, margarine, bread, processed meats and cheeses. (See Salt, page 198 for more details.)

Some foods, particularly breakfast cereals and milk products, include a nutritional information chart listing the number of kilojoules, the amount of protein, fat, starch, sugar, minerals and dietary fibre per serving portion. This information can be useful but don't be misled into thinking that there is a specific benefit from the amount of a particular nutrient in the product.

The advantages and disadvantages of nutritional labelling, and ways of changing regulations to make food labelling more in accord with modern dietary guidelines, are currently the subject of intense debate. No doubt the next few years will bring new information on packages to digest before we tuck in!

Contact the manufacturer if the food label does not tell you what you want to know. Most manufacturers are very helpful.

Action to take:
Read labels carefully before putting processed foods into your shopping trolley.

- An understanding of how to interpret labels will help you to better organise your healthy eating regime. You'll be less likely to sprinkle sugar on your favourite breakfast cereal if you appreciate that it already has a *high* sugar content!
- Check labels for ingredients that you want to increase or decrease in your diet.
- You don't have to avoid foods because they have long ingredient lists or contain fat, salt or sugar.
- Don't be taken in by emotive-sounding words on labels such as 'full of natural goodness' and 'nutritionally balanced'.

Fruit

Fruit is important as a source of vitamin C — citrus fruits are rich in this vitamin — and of dietary fibre. The pectin in fruit is a type of dietary fibre and is the focus of considerable research. It may prove to be have a special place in the overall picture of dietary fibre.

Retaining the Nutrients:

- Minimise soaking, cutting, chopping and peeling.

- Taste before adding sugar to stewed fruit.
- Bottle fruit in water — sugar is not required to preserve fruit.
- Eat raw rather than cooked fruit where possible.
- Minimise cooking time.

Ways to Prepare and Use Fruit

Apples:
Apples should be crisp and firm. Keep in a plastic bag in the refrigerator.
- Use with cheese as a sandwich filling.
- Slice finely or dice, leaving skins on, and add to tossed salads or coleslaw.
- Stew with sultanas, a little water and some grated lemon rind and cinnamon and use to filled wholemeal pancakes. Top with low-fat natural yoghurt.

Apricots:
Apricots should be firm and brightly coloured. Store in an unsealed plastic bag in the refrigerator. Use as soon as possible.
- Cook with chopped onion and a little vinegar, stirring in chopped mint at the last minute for a tangy sauce to serve with roast meats or curry.
- Blend fresh apricots with orange or apple juice. Add soda or mineral water, a slice of lemon and a mint sprig for a refreshing drink.

Bananas:
Bananas should be pale green or yellow in colour. Ripen at room temperature. For longer storage store in refrigerator — skin will blacken but fruit does not deteriorate as quickly.
- For a milkshake — blend with milk and vanilla essence. Serve chilled in a tall glass. Sprinkle with nutmeg.
- Peel and slice lengthwise into halves. Brush with lemon juice and grill. Serve with meat dishes.
- Barbecue in skins and serve with meat dishes.
- Use as an accompaniment to curries.
- Leave skins on and slice thickly. Arrange attractively with other fresh fruit on a platter.

Cherries:
Cherries should be firm and glossy with stalks still attached. Store in an unsealed plastic bag in the refrigerator for 1 to 2 days.

- Stone cherries and toss among fresh vegetables or fruit in salads for added colour.
- Use in fruit soups such as Spiced Cherry Soup. (See page 67.)

Figs:
Fresh figs should be firm and purple in colour. Store in an unsealed plastic bag in the refrigerator. Use as soon as possible.
- Wash, remove stems and simmer in a little water until just tender. Chill and serve with yoghurt sprinkled with toasted slivered almonds.
- Wash fresh figs. Cut into lengthwise quarters without cutting through base. Open out into a flower shape. Serve chilled as an entrée with a teaspoon of ricotta cheese placed in the centre and chopped walnuts sprinkled over the top.

Grapefruit:
Grapefruit should be firm and heavy with smooth, yellow skin. Can be kept in a cool place for up to two weeks and in refrigerator for longer storage.
- Cut in half, loosen segments and serve fresh or grilled lightly. Top with mint sprigs.
- Peel and cut into slices, place in a bowl and cover with apple juice. Sprinkle with finely chopped mint. Chill and serve with yoghurt for breakfast.
- Peel grapefruit and cut into segments. Add to tossed salad.

Grapes:
Grapes should be firm and plump with fruit firmly attached to stems. Keep in an unsealed plastic bag in the refrigerator and use as quickly as possible.
- Freeze in bunches for an iced summer snack.
- Add to honeydew melon and rockmelon for a light entrée or dessert.
- For Fresh Fruit Kebabs — skewer green and black grapes alternately with thick banana slices, wedges of rock melon, strawberries and cubes of pineapple.

Lemons:
Lemons should be firm and heavy with fine textured skins. Store at room temperature.
- Squeeze lemons and freeze juice in ice-cube trays. Remove when frozen and keep in plastic bags in freezer for use in sauces, drinks and fruit salads.
- Freeze whole lemons, defrost and squeeze for juice.

- Use lemon juice in salad dressings instead of vinegar.
- Add lemon juice to apples, avocados, pears and bananas to prevent discolouring.

Mandarins:
Mandarins should be firm and heavy with glossy skins. Store in a cool place or in refrigerator for longer storage.
- Poach segments lightly in water and vinegar. Use as a garnish for meat or fish dishes.

Mangoes:
Mangoes should be firm with an orange tinge and free from blemishes. Keep at room temperature until ripe and then in refrigerator.
- Peel fruit and remove flesh. Blend either on its own or with a little natural low-fat yoghurt or use as a sauce for fruit salad.
- Serve wedges on a fruit platter with ricotta cheese.
- Peel and remove flesh. Dice and add to fruit salad for a delicious tropical flavour.
- Use in chutneys.

Nectarines:
Nectarines should be brightly coloured, smooth and plump. Refrigerate ripe fruit and use as soon as possible.
- Slice fresh fruit into a bowl. Chill. Serve with muesli and yoghurt for breakfast.
- Use sliced in wholemeal bread sandwiches with a little low-fat cream cheese.
- Stew nectarines without sugar. Use as a dessert or freeze for later use.

Oranges:
Oranges should be firm and heavy with glossy skins. Will keep in a cool place for approximately two weeks, but should be refrigerated for longer storage.
- Use orange segments or slices in salads.
- Serve orange slices with pork dishes instead of apple sauce.
- Poach in spiced vinegar and use as an accompaniment to meat dishes. Use small Valencias as they are easy to handle.
- It is better to eat an orange than drink orange juice — you get more fibre and fewer kilojoules.

Pawpaw:
Pawpaw should be brightly coloured and free of bruising.

194

Ripen at room temperature, and then store in refrigerator. Use as soon as possible.

- Use in fruit salads, or slice and serve with other tropical fruits on a fruit platter.

Passionfruit:
Passionfruit should be smooth and deep purple. Keep in crisper in refrigerator.

- Freeze pulp in ice-cube trays. Remove and keep in a plastic bag in the deep freeze. Use for punch or for fruit salad.
- Add passionfruit pulp to fruit-whip drinks for an extra tangy flavour.

Peaches:
Peaches should be firm and just beginning to soften. Store in an unsealed plastic bag in the refrigerator.

- Peel and serve on lightly buttered wholemeal bread.
- Simmer with lemon peel and cinnamon.
- Grill peach halves and serve with roast chicken.

Pears:
Pears should be firm and free from bruising. Ripen at room temperature. Store in an unsealed plastic bag in the refrigerator.

- Peel, core and quarter. Poach in white wine or apple juice, adding cloves to taste.
- Eat fresh with ricotta cheese.
- Poach pears lightly in a little water. Chill and serve with puréed raspberries.

Pineapple:
Pineapple should be firm, with a bright-coloured skin and have a pleasant aroma. Pineapple is ripe enough to eat if leaves can be easily removed. Store in a cool place or refrigerate.

- Serve on a fruit platter, cut into quarters with the skin still intact for easy handling.
- Scrape flesh from pineapple and add to fruit drinks.

Plums:
Plums should be smooth, brightly-coloured and with no sign of wrinkling. Ripen at room temperature. Store in an unsealed bag in the refrigerator.

- Plums make a delicious fruit soup, stewed with water or wine and water mixed, spices, lemon peel and a little tapioca. Add sugar to taste.

- Stew fruit with slices of green ginger and a little sugar to taste. Remove ginger and chill. Serve sprinkled with toasted almonds and natural low-fat yoghurt.

Raspberries:
Raspberries should be firm, whole and deep red in colour. Store in the refrigerator, but use as quickly as possible as they perish.
- Mix fresh raspberries with your muesli and milk for breakfast — the season is short so enjoy the luxury!
- Add raspberries to fruit whip drinks.
- Stir raspberries through fruit salad at the last minute to prevent them becoming mushy.

Rockmelon:
Melons should have no soft spots. A good aroma indicates ripeness. Store in the refrigerator when ripe. Wrap cut melon in plastic.
- Cut into quarters, remove seeds. Sprinkle with lemon juice and powdered ginger. Serve as an entrée, a dessert or a snack.
- Dice or scoop out melon balls and add mint and lemon juice.

Strawberries:
Strawberries should be clean, bright red in colour with no signs of mould and no soft spots. Store in refrigerator and use as quickly as possible as they perish.
- Add to fruit salads and punches.
- Purée strawberries and use as a fruit sauce.
- Blend fresh strawberries with milk and a little vanilla for a delicious milkshake.
- Serve fresh, whole, unhulled strawberries on a platter lined with grape leaves.

Watermelon:
Watermelons should be large with deep-pink flesh. A pale yellow underside on the skin indicates ripeness. Store in a cool place and refrigerate when cut. Use as soon as possible as the flesh loses its crispness.
- Serve in wedges on a hot day.
- Add to fruit salad for extra colour and delicious crispness.
- Dice fruit, removing seeds. Place in a bowl and add finely sliced onion rings. Add a dressing of oil, lemon juice and black pepper. Chill and serve with hot or cold meats or cheese.

> ### Action to take:
> Include fruit in some form in all meals.
>
> - Fruit makes a substantial contribution to the pleasure of eating and the art of living. No other class of foods contributes such a variety of attractive flavours, textures and colours.
> - Choose fresh fruit as an alternative to fatty and sugary desserts because it has a low energy density.
> - Take advantage of the versatility of fruit and use fresh, or in stewed desserts, fruit soups, juices, sauces, spreads and chutneys.
> - Use fruit to garnish meat and to combine with vegetables in salads.
> - Substitute out of season fruit with unsweetened canned, frozen or dried fruits.

Health Foods

Ironically the modern focus on health foods gathered momentum as a direct result of the increasing modification and manipulation of foods in the late 1940s and in the 1950s. During this period there was a proliferation of processed foods as new products were developed to please the palate, dazzle the eye and ease the task of food preparation.

The growing consumer movement of the 1960s attacked the food industry for adding, in the words of a former US politician, 'all those unsafe, untested, unnecessary chemicals to our food supply'. The health food industry developed rapidly in tandem with food activism, and produced the idea that the word 'health' in association with the word 'food' means that the food to which this description is applied is in some way different to 'ordinary' food. In other words, that this type of food can lead to a state of well-being beyond that given by food which does *not* have the prefix 'health'.

Since the start of this decade there has been a growing awareness that the term 'health' should be linked to the total diet and not to specific foods. A healthy diet is made up of 'ordinary' foods from Rows 1 and 2 of the Healthy Diet Triangle, eaten liberally and regularly because of their nutritional properties and their low content of less desirable constituents.

Action to take:
Use the Healthy Diet Triangle as a basis for selecting some foods sold in health food shops to increase variety in your diet.

- Although health food stores stock products which may be unavailable elsewhere don't assume that everything sold in these shops is necessarily health-promoting.

What to Buy in Health Food Shops

- Grains and cereal products — to make muesli, bread, muffins, rice and pasta dishes. (See Chapter 3 for recipes.)
- Legumes — such as soya flour, miso (fermented soya bean paste) and tofu (soya bean curd) as well as a range of dried beans and peas.
- Seeds, nuts and dried fruits — to add to a meal of grains and vegetables or to muesli.

Once inside the health food store be on your guard about eye-catching labels such as 'organic' and 'natural'. There is no general agreement on what these terms mean nor whether foods which are given these adjectives are safer and more nutritious than conventionally grown and marketed foods. Many fables abound such as the claim that natural vitamins are superior to synthetic vitamins (they have identical chemical structures), that the soil is 'all worn out' or that organic fertilisers result in better crops than manufactured fertilisers (a plant will only grow if there are adequate nutrients in the soil — its composition does not depend on the source of the nutrients).

Salt

Sodium and **salt** are not one and the same thing. Salt is made from two chemical elements, sodium (40 per cent) and chlorine (60 per cent). To convert sodium content to salt (sodium chloride) equivalent, multiply the figure for sodium by 2.5.

A daily intake of less than 2000 milligrams of **sodium** has been recommended. This is equivalent to approximately 5 grams of salt or one teaspoon. Many people eat more than double this amount without being aware of doing so. This is in spite of the fact one gram of **salt** is sufficient for the body's needs. Be assured that it's almost impossible to have an inadequate intake of salt.

Sources of Sodium

Surveys of which foods are the major contributors of sodium in the diet, apart from the salt added to food in cooking or at the table, have revealed the following:

Processed food	Sodium in diet
• Bread and breakfast cereals	25–40 per cent
• Processed meats such as bacon, ham, sausages and corned beef	27–38 per cent
• Butter, margarine and cheese	16 per cent
• Milk	7 per cent
• Soups and salty spreads	5–12 per cent
Unprocessed food	
• Vegetables	6 per cent
• Fruit	trace

Would you have thought that such a large proportion of dietary sodium comes from bread and cereals?

Other sources of sodium are:

- Bicarbonate of soda — used in baking.
- Sodium nitrite — added as a preservative to some meat products.
- Monosodium glutamate — used as a flavour enhancer especially in Chinese cooking.

The Healthy Diet Triangle is to some extent a guide to low-salt eating. The foods in the top two rows don't contain much salt in themselves. It's what's done to them in the factory or kitchen that can bump up the salt content. Fresh meats, for example,

199

are lower in sodium than processed meats such as bacon, ham and sausages, all of which have had sodium added to flavour and preserve them. Many of us from habit add salt to food during cooking and then use a salt shaker at the table.

Action to take:
If you have high blood pressure or if there is a history of the disease in your immediate family then reduce the amount of salt you eat.

- A reduced salt intake is often sufficient to lower blood pressure to a healthy range. It can also increase the effectiveness of anti-hypertensive drug treatment, making a lower dosage possible.
- If your blood pressure is in the healthy range — you can readily check with your doctor — and if there is no family history of hypertension then you don't have to worry about reducing your own salt intake.
- Some of the people for whom you prepare food may benefit from a low-salt diet. Salty foods dull the palate's sensitivity to delicate and subtle flavouring.
- A low-salt diet can be interesting if you develop the style of eating outlined in this book and try the recipes. Read food labels on processed foods carefully.

Ways to Reduce Salt Intake

- Find out which foods in general contain less sodium.
- Look for low-sodium and sodium-free items when shopping for groceries. There is an increasing number of products available which have substantially less sodium than they had previously. Among these are breads, breakfast cereals, butter and margarine. If salt is one of the first three ingredients listed, the product is high in sodium.
- Gradually reduce the amount of salt you use each day when cooking meals at home. Experiment with flavours which can substitute for salt such as lemon juice, herbs, spices, onion and garlic powder (not salt), powdered mustard, finely chopped garlic and freshly grated horseradish.

- Try chewing food more thoroughly if it tastes blander than before. Chewing breaks down food and allows more molecules to interact with taste receptors in the mouth. You may also find that it helps to alternate bites of different foods. When you eat several bites of the same food, the flavour is stronger in the first bite than the subsequent ones.
- Choose items that are unlikely to have large amounts of salt added when eating out. Many restaurants will prepare low-sodium meals on request.

A Case Study

Ken was a very fit, lean man. He was a farmer who also did some building in a nearby country town and was always on the go and seldom ill. Then at age 70, right out of the blue, he had a massive stroke. It seemed that he was going to be paralysed down one side of his body and would never walk again. Yet he made a remarkable physical recovery and within a few months was able to walk almost normally. But his speech wasn't normal. His words came out in a jumble and it was desperately sad to see his tears of frustration because he was unable to say what he wanted.

Ken, like many farmers, kept his cars and tractors in good order. But he didn't have a regular check that his body was also in good working order. Further, he ate a lot of salt, as did his children and teenage grandchildren. They all firmly believed that people who live in hot climates should eat plenty of salt.

It's very likely that Ken's stroke was due to an excess intake of salt over a long period. There is clear evidence that hypertension (high blood pressure) in some people is linked to a high salt intake. It is also well established that the body has very efficient mechanisms for conserving salt and so it's not necessary to consume any more when living in a hot climate. Symptoms attributed to lack of salt are much more likely due to dehydration or loss of water from body tissues.

Supplements — Vitamins and Minerals

> ## *Action to take:*
> Use supplements only as a last resort.
>
> - Most people in the vital years can get all the nutrients they need if they eat a wide range of nutritious foods each day, in the quantities suggested on page 40. Use of supplements tends to divert attention from the benefits which can be achieved from developing a dietary pattern based on Rows 1 and 2 of the Healthy Diet Triangle.
> - Take with a pinch of salt(!) claims by advertisers of vitamin and mineral supplements that their products will improve physical appearance, give sex life a boost, prevent or cure disease and lengthen life. There is little scientific evidence to support most of these claims.
> - Beware of buzz words frequently used about supplements, words such as 'revolutionary breakthrough', 'medically proven', 'nutritional first' and 'optimum health', particularly if no comprehensive dietary advice is provided in conjunction with recommendations on how to use the products. Just imagine how many products might claim to have 'awesome' healing powers now that it has become a vogue word. Remember the constant reference to the 'awesome' speed and crew work of *Stars and Stripes* in the Americas Cup? How could we forget!

What are Food Supplements?

They are specially formulated, non-food preparations made up of substances such as vitamins, minerals, amino acids, lecithins or enzymes, or combinations of these or other ingredients. They are sold over the counter as tablets, capsules, pills, wafers, powders or liquids.

Are Supplements of Value?

Until the past few decades food was the body's only source of nutrients. Today nutrients can also be provided by food supplements.

There is only one way to ascertain whether a healthy person who eats a balanced diet can benefit from nutritional supplements. This is to assess their effectiveness and possible toxicity in long-term studies. This research has not yet been done. Some nutrition experts doubt that our bodies would function better when provided with higher doses of vitamins and minerals than can be supplied from food. They argue that this situation has not existed in nature, that a varied diet contains more nutrients than our bodies can use and that any excess is of no benefit — and may even be dangerous in the case of fat-soluble vitamins A and D.

There is no scientific evidence to show that specially formulated supplements help to overcome alleged dangers from stressful lifestyles, environmental pollution and the depletion of nutrients from modern farming and food processing methods, as claimed by manufacturers of these supplements.

The trouble with supplements is where to begin and where to end. By the time you've started on multivitamins, multiminerals, calcium, fish oil concentrates and fibre supplements, for example, there's a good chance that you will have upset the balance of nutrients in your food. And you might still be missing something!

You are likely to benefit substantially more from a dietary pattern based on Rows 1 and 2 of the Healthy Diet Triangle than one which is dependent on supplements. Supplements, such as a low-dose multivitamin preparation, may be of value in circumstances such as prolonged illness or where it is impossible to eat a balanced diet because there is no access to a range of nutritious foods.

Vegetables

The main nutritional contributions of vegetables to the diet are vitamin C (ascorbic acid), folic acid (one of the B group of vitamins) and dietary fibre. Green leafy vegetables are also useful sources of calcium and beta-carotene, the precursor of vitamin A.

Retaining the Nutrients:
• Prepare as close as possible to cooking and eating.

- Minimise soaking, cutting, chopping and peeling.
- Minimise cooking time.
- Steam or microwave when cooking to retain colour, flavour and nutrient content.
- Avoid using bicarbonate of soda to intensify green colour in vegetables as it destroys vitamin C and folic acid.

Action to take:

Vegetables should make the bulk of your mid-day or evening meal.

- Increase the amount of vegetables and decrease the quantity of meat in savoury dishes. Meat should be served as an accompaniment to vegetables rather than the other way round.
- Although there's nothing quite like the flavour of home-grown vegetables, which can be eaten as soon as picked, there are attractive alternatives available in the market place. High quality produce at the greengrocer, combined with the wide range of frozen out-of-season vegetables at the supermarket, provide the vegetable lover with a marvellous opportunity for experimentation.
- Use vegetables as the mainstay of a weight-control diet because they are low in kilojoules and high in bulk.

Ways to Prepare and Use Vegetables

Alfalfa sprouts:

Alfalfa can be brought already sprouted or you can sprout it yourself. Seeds can be obtained from most health-food stores. Place 1 dessertspoon seeds in hot water in a glass jar — cover with plastic and leave to soak for 6–8 hours. Strain and rinse with cold water. Rinse once or twice each day until sprouts are required length — this will take approximately 3–4 days.
- Use in salads, sandwiches and soups.

Asparagus:

Asparagus should be firm with green tops. Store in refrigerator in unsealed plastic bag.
- Cut diagonally in 5 cm (2 in) slices and steam lightly — toss in a little butter or margarine.

- Simmer whole asparagus spears in a little chicken stock for 5 minutes for added flavour.
- Slice diagonally and stir-fry quickly in a little oil.

Avocado:
Avocados are ready to use when just beginning to soften. Store unripe fruit at room temperature and in the refrigerator when ripened.
- Substitute avocado for butter or margarine on bread and top with bean sprouts.
- Slice finely in salads.
- For a summer soup — mash two or three avocados and blend with chicken stock, natural low-fat yoghurt, white wine, chives and black pepper for a delicious cool summer soup.
- Use in dips such as Guacamole. (see page 128.)
- Use as a filler in tacos, the bland flavour complements the spices.

Beans:
Beans should be young, firm and bright green in colour. Store in an unsealed plastic bag in the refrigerator.
- Top and tail and steam whole until just tender. Sprinkle with pine nuts or sunflower seeds, or cool and use in salads.

Bean sprouts:
Bean sprouts should be kept in a screw-top glass jar in the refrigerator.
- Use in stir-fried dishes and salads.
- Add to soup just before serving for crunchiness and extra vitamins.

Beetroot:
Beetroot should be firm and deep purple with green tops still attached to signify freshness.
- Grate raw for sandwiches and salads.
- Wash, cover with water and simmer until just tender. Remove skin, slice or dice. Serve hot or sprinkle with vinegar, cover and refrigerate.

Broccoli:
Broccoli should be firm with dark green heads and no signs of yellowing. Use as soon as possible as it perishes quickly. Store in plastic bag in refrigerator, or blanch and freeze until needed.

- Wash well and cut into small florets. Steam lightly for 3–5 minutes until slightly crisp and bright green. Sprinkle with lemon juice and pepper.
- Cut into small florets and stir-fry, Chinese-style, in a little oil and soy sauce.
- Try broccoli cheese instead of cauliflower cheese. Sprinkle pine nuts over the top before baking.
- Refresh cooked broccoli in iced water, drain, and toss in your favourite dressing.

Brussels sprouts:
Brussels sprouts should be firm, compact and bright green. They only keep for 2–3 days. Store in unsealed plastic bag in refrigerator.
- Steam lightly. Sprinkle with lemon thyme, black pepper and a knob of margarine.
- Boil in a little water for 5–6 minutes — reserve water. Make a sauce using 1 dessertspoon low-salt margarine, 1 dessertspoon flour, reserved liquid made up to 1 cup with milk or stock, black pepper and parsley. Pour over sprouts — delicious!
- Cut sprouts into lengthwise quarters, stir-fry until bright green and just cooked.

Cabbage:
Cabbage should be firm with crisp outer leaves. Wrap in plastic and store in refrigerator.
- Shred and steam lightly with diced, unpeeled, red apple. Sprinkle with a few caraway seeds and lemon juice before serving.
- For cabbage rolls — place a small quantity of cooked minced lamb or veal, rice and herbs on a blanched cabbage leaf. Wrap up securely, steam until tender. Serve with your favourite sauce.
- For a Greek salad — mix with sliced capsicum, diced cucumber, tomato wedges, black olives and feta cheese.
- For a fruity salad — mix with lychees, mandarin segments, sliced mushrooms, sliced celery, slivered almonds, grated ginger root, lemon juice, soy sauce and yoghurt.

Peppers
Peppers should be firm, glossy and bright red or green. Store in an unsealed plastic bag in the refrigerator for up to 1 week.
- Blanch in boiling water for 3 minutes. Cut in half lengthwise, remove seeds and fill with a stuffing of your choice — rice,

206

tomatoes, cheese and mushrooms. Bake 20 minutes in a moderate oven.
- Slice in rings, remove seeds, and use in salads for added colour and texture.
- Cut into cubes and add to spaghetti sauces, casseroles or fried rice.
- Use as a crisp filling in sandwiches.

Carrots:
Carrots should be firm, smooth and brightly coloured. Store in an unsealed plastic bag in the refrigerator.
- Scrub unpeeled carrots, slice diagonally and steam for 10 minutes until just soft. Serve with lemon wedges.
- For a sandwich filling, grate and add to cottage or ricotta cheese, sultanas and beansprouts.

Cauliflower:
Cauliflower should be firm, white and compact. Wrap in plastic film and store in refrigerator.
- Cut into florets, steam lightly. Top with a dob of ricotta cheese, cottage cheese or yoghurt. Sprinkle with chives or chopped nuts.
- Blanch in boiling water for 1 minute. Stir-fry with an assortment of vegetables.
- Serve with a nutmeg-flavoured cheese sauce.

Celery:
Celery should be crisp with light green stalks and a light-coloured butt. Store in an unsealed plastic bag in the refrigerator.
- Try celery pieces filled with crunchy peanut butter for a delicious snack!
- Cut stalks into 5 cm (2 in) lengths, steam for 5 minutes. Serve with a light cheese sauce.

Corn cobs:
Corn cobs should be fresh, light yellow in colour and free of unwrinkled kernels.
- Cook corn in rapidly boiling water for 3−5 minutes. Serve with butter or margarine and black pepper.
- Barbecue whole in the husk for 15−20 minutes.
- Remove kernels with a sharp knife and use in soups, sauces or salads.

Cucumber:
Cucumber should be firm and green, with no signs of yellowing. Store in vegetable crisper in the refrigerator.
- Poach long strips of cucumber in 1/4 cup vinegar, 1/4 cup water, a knob of margarine and 1 teaspoon brown sugar for 20 minutes, turning occasionally. Serve hot.
- Delicious in sandwiches — especially with low-fat cream cheese which has been mixed with chopped fresh herbs.
- Use in summer soups.

• Aubergine:
Aubergine should be firm and dark purple with glossy skin. Store in vegetable crisper in the refrigerator for a week to 10 days.
- For ratatouille — slice and sprinkle with salt. Leave for 1/2 hour to remove bitter juices. Wash and pat dry. Simmer with sliced tomatoes, onions, courgettes and peppers. Add tomato flakes, chopped parsley and marjoram. Serve hot or cold.
- Stuff with mince and rice and bake in moderate oven.
- Grill aubergine, which has been lightly brushed with oil, instead of frying for dishes such as moussaka.

Garlic:
Garlic bulbs should be firm and dry. Store in a cool dry place.
- Use crushed garlic in salad dressings, sauces, soups and marinades.
- Rub a whole clove over meat, chicken or fish for a light garlic flavour.

Leeks:
Leeks should have fresh green tops and a firm base. Keep in an unsealed plastic bag in the refrigerator.
- Should be washed thoroughly to remove all traces of dirt.
- Steam leeks which have been cut in 10 cm (4 in) lengths. Serve hot with a sauce made of onions, tomatoes and basil. Sprinkle with cheese.
- Chill cooked leeks and serve with salad dressing.

Lettuce:
Lettuce should be firm and crisp with blemish-free leaves. Keep in a special crisper bowl, wrap in plastic film or keep in an unsealed plastic bag in the refrigerator.
- Shred lettuce finely and stir through clear soups just before serving. Delicious and crunchy!

Mushrooms:
Mushrooms should be firm, white and unbroken. Store in a paper bag in the refrigerator for a few days only.
- For mushroom salad — select small, firm mushrooms, wash and pat dry. Add chopped parsley and chives. Toss in French dressing.
- Remove stems and wash. Fill with a mixture of low-fat cream cheese, sunflower seeds and chives. Sprinkle with paprika and grill until cheese softens — approximately 5 minutes. Serve with salad and crusty rolls.
- Slice thinly and add to fried rice.
- Delicious in pasta sauces.

Onions:
Onions should be hard with dry skins and no sign of sprouting. Store in a cool, dry and dark place.
- For salads — to remove strong flavour, slice onions finely and place in strainer. Pour boiling water over onions. Cool for 1 minute in iced water. Strain and pat dry.
- Barbecue whole in skins.
- Layer onions and potato slices in a deep casserole, sprinkling pepper between each layer. Half fill casserole with milk. Bake in a moderate oven for approximately 1 hour or until tender.

Parsnips:
Parsnips should be firm and smooth. Keep in a vegetable crisper in the refrigerator.
- Scrub parsnips, slice finely and steam 10 minutes until just tender. Sprinkle with chopped thyme.
- Cook with carrots and mash together. Serve with a small knob of margarine.

Peas:
Fresh peas should be bright green with crisp pods. Keep in an unsealed plastic bag in vegetable crisper in refrigerator. Use within a week.
- Steam lightly and add pine nuts and chopped mint.
- For a quick pea soup — add peas and slice of ham to chicken stock and simmer for 2 minutes. Purée in food processor and serve hot or cold.
- Add snow peas to salads.
- Stir-fry snow peas with vegetables in Chinese dishes.

Potatoes:
Potatoes should be firm, free of green areas, sprouts and blemishes. Store in a cool, dark, dry place. They can also be
stored in the refrigerator.

- For low-fat 'roast' potatoes — scrub whole potatoes, leaving
  skins on. Cut in half and lay cut-side down in a lightly oiled
  baking dish. Bake 3/4-1 hour in a moderate oven. The bottoms
  will be crunchy and the tops fat-free.
- Add low-fat grated cheese and chopped chives or parsley
  when mashing potatoes.
- Scoop out centre of baked jacket potatoes and fill with tasty
  ingredients of your choice. Return to oven and bake for a
  further 10–15 minutes.

Pumpkin:
Store uncut pumpkin in a cool, dry place. Wrap cut pumpkin
in plastic film and store in crisper in refrigerator.

- Steam, peeled or unpeeled for 15–20 minutes. Mash and serve
  sprinkled with nutmeg.
- Use for pumpkin scones, muffins or cakes.
- Stuff and bake. (See Stuffed Butternut Pumpkin page 102.)

Spinach and silverbeet:
Leaves should be glossy and bright green. Wrap in plastic film
and store in refrigerator. Use as soon as possible.

- Wash leaves well. Shake off excess water and place in a
  saucepan with only the water left on the leaves. Cover and
  cook over a moderate heat until the spinach 'collapses'. Drain
  and chop. Add slivered almonds and lemon juice.
- Use young, tender raw leaves in salads. Add cooked chopped
  crisp bacon pieces for extra flavour.
- Purée and add to cheese sauce for pasta dishes.

Sweet potatoes:
Sweet potatoes should be firm and free of sprouts. Store in a
cool, dark, dry place, or in vegetable crisper in refrigerator.

- Cut into rings and steam until transparent.
- Bake whole in skins.

Tomatoes:
Tomatoes should be a bright red colour and free of blemishes.
Store unripe fruit at room temperature until ready for use. Ripe
fruit should be stored in vegetable crisper in refrigerator.

- For tomatoes on toast — slice tomatoes. Add thinly sliced onions, a dash of white wine, bay leaf and fresh chopped basil. Simmer until liquid is reduced.
- Cut tops off tomatoes. Scoop out seeds and fill with mixture of breadcrumbs, chopped onions, mushrooms, sunflower seeds and chopped parsley.

Courgettes:
Courgettes should be firm with glossy skins and free of blemishes. Store in an unsealed bag in refrigerator.
- Grate courgettes and shred equal quantity of lettuce. Cook together quickly in a frying pan with a small knob of butter until just tender. Sprinkle with black pepper and add a squeeze of lemon juice.
- Slice finely and add raw to sandwiches or salads.

Weight Control

When you make your new start it's worth considering whether your weight is a problem. Are you overweight or underweight? Is your weight preventing you from doing the things you want because you feel unwell, tired or lack confidence in your appearance?

Successful weight control is based on using the Healthy Diet Triangle as a focus for good nutrition and health.

Overweight

Approximately one third of Australians will suffer from overweight or obesity as they get older. If you're one of this group you'll probably have tried a variety of ways to lose weight and you might have given up in despair. Well, help is at hand!

There are a number of factors to consider about the precise value to you of making the effort to lose weight.

Your health:
How can you tell if your weight is affecting your health? It is if you have difficulty with everyday activities. You get puffed quickly when climbing stairs, your knees ache, you can't bend

over — these are just some of the physical restrictions which go hand in hand with being overweight.

Excess weight is also linked to illnesses such as diabetes, high blood pressure, varicose veins and haemorrhoids. The most effective way to prevent these conditions is to lose weight. You increase your risk of suffering from heart disease if you are overweight, particularly if you smoke, have high blood fats or high blood pressure.

You can check if you are in the healthy weight range from the chart. If the answer is yes then your weight is unlikely to lead to ill health.

Your looks:
Let's face it. Once we're into our forties or older we're not going to regain the sylph-like figures of our twenties. But what we can achieve is that certain style which comes from inner confidence and poise rather than youthful looks.

If you maintain your weight, or perhaps lose a little, you may feel more confident about your appearance and more adventurous in your choice of clothes.

Your physical performance:
Confronting new challenges in life, whether it be in the home or work environment, could necessitate more physical activity than has been the case in the past few years. You may decide to take up bush walking or dancing or to spend more time playing cricket or going fishing with your children or grand-children. You might take on a task that requires physical exertion, such as looking after children! Losing some weight could be crucial if you are to perform these activities without too much strain.

How to Lose Weight Successfully

Here is the key to success if you are determined to lose weight. Watch very carefully the amount of fat you eat, because fat is such a rich source of calories and is so difficult to detect in foods, as explained in the section on fat. (See page 46.)

This might sound too simple. It's not! However, if you use the Healthy Diet Triangle as your guide you will reduce your fat intake and increase your intake of complex carbohydrates (see page 172). And if you stick to Row 1 and Row 2 foods, using the recipes in this book and undertake a program of regular, enjoyable exercise (see page 184), you will lose weight — slowly (up to 0.5 kg or 1 lb per week) but consistently.

Weight for Height Graph

Weight in kilograms (pounds) — in light clothing

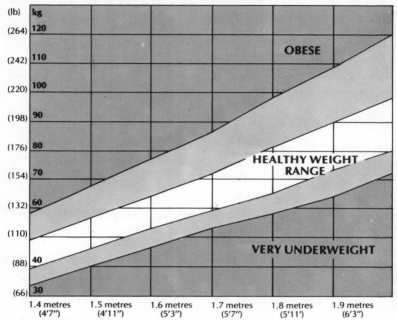

Height in metres (feet and inches) — without shoes

Handy hints:

- Have a particular goal in mind before you try to lose weight — apart from the amount of weight you want to lose. It should be something you can plan with a sense of pleasurable anticipation, like a holiday.
- Work out precisely how much weight you want to lose. Make a chart with an expected rate of loss of not more than 0.5 kg or 1 lb per week, on average. A hardheaded, calm approach to weight control, with good nutrition and good health always in mind, is most likely to bring the results you want.
- Make up a menu plan according to the Healthy Diet Triangle and concentrate on eating mainly Row 1 foods to achieve a daily intake of not more than 1200 calories (5000 kilojoules) — and stick to it.
- Start some daily exercises such as walking or swimming and increase the pace as your fitness improves.

- Develop new strategies for handling stress. One of the problems many overweight people face is that they tend to eat when frustrated or stressed in some way. Work out a strategy so that when you feel stressed, you take a walk, do some deep breathing or turn on some music.
- Be patient. You won't lose weight dramatically. If you do, it's probably a bad sign because it often means you are undereating and will sooner or later become fed up with feeling so hungry and regain weight. Make your new eating pattern part of your new philosophy to achieve good health.

Underweight

If you are underweight it can also prevent you from achieving what you want. Thin people run the risk of lower resistance to infection and constant fatigue; they also take longer to recover from illness.

Eat the following foods in generous quantities to gain weight:
- Butter or margarine on your bread, rolls, rice, potatoes and vegetables.
- Cheese on bread, as a snack with biscuits, in casseroles and in sauces for vegetables and meats.
- Sour cream in casseroles and soups.
- Cream with fruit salad.
- Nuts and dried fruits as snacks — keep these handy so that they're always within reach.

  Again, don't be in a hurry. You'll put on weight gradually once you develop an adventuresome approach to food and a pattern of eating which incorporates the extras mentioned above. You can ease off the high-fat regime once you've made the gain you want.

Your Check List

This is a list that you might like to look at periodically to remind yourself of where changes are still required in your diet.

Changes made over the past ... months:

- Eat more vegetables.
- Eat more fruit.
- Serve fruit as dessert.
- Serve smaller portions of meat.
- Eat fish more often.
- Use low-fat milk.
- Use high-fibre bread (including wholemeal).
- Use wholemeal flour in baked products such as scones.
- Use brown rice and wholemeal pasta noodles.
- Modify favourite dishes, baked goods, cakes and so on by reducing the sugar content.
- Reduce use of salt.
- Combine cottage cheese and matured cheese in recipes, such as sauces.
- Use herbs for flavouring.
- Eat more vegetarian meals.
- Drink more fluid.

Index